Best wishes
Mike Gray

RONNIE BIGGS:
THE INSIDE STORY

RONNIE BIGGS: THE INSIDE STORY

Mike Gray and Tel Currie

Foreword by Michael Biggs

APEX PUBLISHING LTD

Hardback first published in 2008 by

Apex Publishing Ltd
PO Box 7086, Clacton on Sea, Essex, CO15 5WN, England
www.apexpublishing.co.uk

Copyright © 2008 by Mike Gray and Tel Currie
The authors have asserted their moral rights

British Library Cataloguing-in-Publication Data
A catalogue record for this book
is available from the British Library

ISBN HARDBACK: 1-906358-59-1   978-1-906358-59-4

Typeset in 10.5pt Gill Sans MT

Production Manager: Chris Cowlin

Cover Design: Siobhan Smith

Printed by the MPG Books Group in the UK

This book is dedicated to:
Harry Marsden, Joey Pyle Snr and Tel Currie Snr

INTRODUCTION
by Mike Gray

Since Ronnie's return to England in 2001, myself and Tel have visited him in both HMP Belmarsh and HMP Norwich and are still doing so today. Ronnie has had a very rough ride since landing back in Blighty, serving six years in the UK's most secure prison with the strictest security regime you can ever imagine. In this book we tell of our visits, which were sometimes unpleasant and heartbreaking, but during which we had to stay strong for Ronnie.

Ronnie is 79-years-old, totally wheelchair bound, has no speech, cannot write, needs assistance to go to the toilet, is fed via a tube into his stomach and has poor overall health, yet he is still imprisoned in Category C HMP Norwich. We wrote our book to make the public aware of the conditions he is living under and his current situation, which is bordering on grave. As I have always said: "Ronnie Biggs is being slowly crucified on the Home Office Cross." The time has come, to take him down.

Best regards,
Mike Gray

INTRODUCTION
by Tel Currie

I have mentioned before that I worry about a so-called democracy that can keep a sick old man behind bars whilst sending young men and women in their prime to the other side of the world to be killed!

There are no morals when money is involved. As the genius Roger Waters of Pink Floyd wrote, 'It all makes perfect sense, put into dollars pounds, shillings and pence!'

My great friend, Mike Gray, and I will not be silenced by the propaganda of the upper classes. The world needs more Mike Gray's and Chris Cowlin's - men with balls who will not accept a medieval Britain because it's easier to watch EastEnders and let others do it!

Ronnie Biggs, along with Kevin Lane, Ian McAteer, Willy Gage and God knows how many more men, who are being treated like the animal in the zoo that nobody wants to see.

Ronnie Biggs is being treated like an animal - WE HAVE SEEN IT!

When will people wake up and realise that the police and lawmakers are NOT always right? It's time to stop taking everything at face value and swallowing everything they want us to swallow. For all these men enough is enough!

But don't tut and do nothing, do something. It may be you one day; it's not only career criminals that end up in prison you know, sometimes they're not even criminals at all, the 'Guildford four' and 'Birmingham six' spring to mind. This is everyone's concern. The point of prison is to reform somebody NOT destroy them.

How much more reformed can you get than to be robbed of your speech, unable to eat, hardly able to walk, nearly 80 years old and have suffered countless strokes? Is it possible for someone to be reformed any more than that? I don't think so.

Here we will tell you what happens inside our prisons and dispel the Biggs' myth. The 'Britain has the best justice system in the world' mob may not like what they read but, if it awakens one person from their flag waving dream, the book has succeeded.

And to Ronnie, a non-violent, lovable rogue.... WE LOVE YOU MATE!

Respect,
Tel Currie

FOREWORD
By Michael Biggs

This book is an inside view of my father's life in HMP Belmarsh and HMP Norwich from 2001 to the present date.

Mike Gray and Tel Currie are two among very few people who have first-hand knowledge of my father's life inside Her Majesty's Prisons. It's a real eye opener into the harsh regime my father has had to endure for the past seven-plus years.

I have known Mike Gray since he first contacted my father in 1989, and we have been friends ever since.

Friend (noun): A person whom you know well and whom you like a lot, but who is usually not a member of your family.

The above can sum up my personal feelings for Mike Gray.

Once you are in the spotlight there is no shortage of hangers-on who will always be there for your 15 minutes. Once those are up they disappear like there's no tomorrow.

Unlike most of the idiots who come up once in a while, Mike is always there, in the background; not wanting any attention, not after money or media recognition, and with a loving family who respect and support his admiration for, and friendship with, my father.

Mike has become different from a friend over the years; he has become more than that, and we consider him part of the family.

Like all friends we have had our differences and always will – that is what friends are all about!

When mention of this book came to me my first thought was: if anyone has the right to tell the story of his long-term friendship with Ronnie Biggs, that is surely Mike Gray!

With all of the Biggsy family love

Michael Biggs

Chapter 1
To Free or Not to Free
(by Tel Currie)

"I always said I'll only find out who my true friends are if I'm banged up back in England. Along with my son Michael, Tel Currie, Roy Shaw and Mike Gray are my most regular visitors. They are true friends who stand by me through thick and thin." - Ronnie Biggs

When Roy Shaw and myself went along with our pal Mike Gray to visit Ronnie Biggs in HMP Belmarsh back in 2002, we really didn't know what to expect. I had not met the man before he returned to England and Roy hadn't seen him since his 70th birthday bash in Brazil in 1999. Ronnie had gone seriously downhill since then and had suffered a number of strokes. I am not a ghoulish person in that way and didn't want to see a shell of a man just to be able to tell everyone I had met Ronnie Biggs. I know people who are like that, but thankfully I inherited a great deal of respect.

Ronnie was physically in a very bad way, no doubt about that, but one thing he still has that struck us all is his humour. Ronnie can no longer talk. He has a laminated chart of letters that he points to and spells out the words. The first thing he asked us using his chart was: "Did you come on the train? Ha ha." Ron also took great pleasure in winding Roy up by spelling out that a certain screw or con was calling him a big sissy. Roy would then get the hump asking which one had said it and Ronnie would be cracking up laughing.

However, behind the smiles you could sense the pain. When receiving visitors, he would stare into space during conversation. He showed us the tube that has been inserted into his stomach, which was Ronnie's only way of being fed. His mechanics are uncoordinated, he dribbles constantly and he has extreme trouble walking. But the warmth of the man is incredible. He tries to laugh, he tries to play with the children, and he tries to spread happiness despite his difficulties. Even if Ronnie were young, fit and well, he wouldn't strike you as dangerous or violent. A cheeky monkey or rascal - yes. A dangerous, violent man - no way!

Ronnie was not a violent, dangerous man in 1963 let alone in 2008. Yet this frail, sick old man is still in maximum security HMP Norwich, all paid for by the taxpayers. Why? Do they seriously consider him an escape risk? It doesn't take much working out why Ronnie is being treated like this. It's obvious to me and many others that the reason is politics. Only a brave politician will let Biggsy out and I'm afraid 'a brave politician' is a contradiction in terms. Ronnie Biggs represents a nightmare for them. He's a very famous man who has strong support all over the world. I don't actually think they know what the hell to do with him. He's not a killer; in fact the so-called Great Train Robbery was an unarmed robbery.

Freddie Foreman points out that the ridiculous sentences handed out to the Train Robbers was one of the biggest mistakes in the history of the British justice system: "All the chaps who worked on the pavement said, hang on a minute, if they have been given 30 years, the maximum sentence they can dish out, and they weren't even armed, what's the point of being unarmed? We may as well carry guns; they can't give you a higher sentence and you have more chance of getting the prize with a gun. And if the police shoot we can shoot back. It would be stupid not to carry a shooter because they can't give you any more than the unarmed Train Robbers got. It was a huge mistake. Nobody went out on a job without shooters after that!"

Of course, Fred is right. The handling of the Great Train Robbery started off the whole armed robbery phenomenon of the late 60s, 70s and 80s. The media magic/curse also cast its spell on Ronnie. Ronnie Biggs is a household name; everybody has heard of 'Ronnie Biggs the Great Train

Robber'. But in truth Ronnie wasn't really much of a train robber at all. Ronnie was a carpenter at the time and his old friend Bruce Reynolds was planning the big one. Bruce, who was one of the top blaggers in London and highly respected, had already pulled off a number of spectacular jobs. Biggsy was not in Bruce's league or indeed in any of the others. Men like Charlie Wilson, Buster Edwards, Roger Cordrey, Tommy Wisbey and Gordon Goody were experienced at their jobs.

Ronnie Biggs's one and only asset was that he knew a train driver. Unfortunately, Ronnie's train driver had trouble operating the new type of train controls; in short, he was more of a liability than a godsend. I remember chatting to Bruce on a couple of occasions about how Biggsy got involved, and he told me that he hadn't wanted Ronnie to go on the job:

"There was no need for him to take that risk, no reason at all. I offered him a good cut just to introduce to me to the backup train driver. He would have been well off and never caught because he would not have physically been part of the job. But Ronnie wanted the buzz and pleaded and pleaded with me until I gave in. The rest is history. He should have listened to me."

Now it's almost impossible for the generations after the Great Train Robbery even to think that Ronnie Biggs was an extremely minor player.

When Ronnie's all-important backup train driver jumped into the driver's seat to take the role of saviour of the day and bring the train to its final resting place for the gang to unload the loot, he couldn't move it! Instead the regular driver, Jack Mills, who had been struck over the head with a cosh, was unceremoniously forced back into the driver's seat to manoeuvre the train the last few hundred yards to the rendezvous point, where the multi-efficient human chains were waiting to unload the sacks into the gang's vehicles. Regarding the coshing of Jack Mills, Bruce say's:

"The guy who did that was not one of our regular troops. He was not one of our tight regular firm but was a friend of somebody. What happened to Jack Mills was not supposed to happen, but why Mr Mills decided to struggle and fight I don't know. If he had accepted it wasn't actually his own train all would have been fine. During the melee, the member of the team with little experience hit him."

In a cruel way, this was a godsend for the law who paraded Mr Mills around on TV with outsized bandages on his head for the world to see. At the start of questions from reporters, Mr Mills would slur and appear disorientated, but a few seconds in he was fine until he realised his role again. In the live interview shown the very next day after the robbery Mr Mills is talking perfectly coherently. During this interview Mr Mills told how one of the robbers had wiped the blood out of eyes and tried to make him comfortable, telling him he would be all right. This man was Charlie Wilson. Obviously later on, when the police caught Charlie, this was kept out of the press as far as possible, as Charlie Wilson was considered to be a hardened, seasoned career criminal and looking after the driver was not the public portrayal they wanted of him or the others.

Something about that interview didn't ring true. Jack Mills was not angry, upset or emotional in any way. The impression that seemed obvious was that Mr Mills had been spoon-fed propaganda that didn't appear to match how he actually felt. Jack Mills also revealed that his assailant said: "If you hadn't have grappled with me I wouldn't have had to hit you." Those are hardly the words of someone out of their head and desperate to inflict violence, are they?

Don't get me wrong, I don't approve of what happened to Jack Mills and I'm certainly not trying to give halos to the Train Robbers, but the truth is never as simple as black and white and to untangle the truth can often be messy.

Jack Mills died seven years later from leukaemia and, predictably, the Train Robbery was blamed for this. I have never heard of anyone contracting leukaemia as a direct result of a bash on the head seven years earlier, and neither has anyone else I've ever asked. I certainly do not want to make light of the death of Jack Mills, and I have the deepest respect and sympathy for the family, but it does seem glaringly apparent that Mr Mills was used shamelessly as a propaganda tool for the authorities. It's something we will never know, but I wonder if Mr Mills himself would have wanted an extremely sick Ronnie Biggs still to be rotting in maximum security at 79 years of age?

Another member of the gang told me:

"Photos of Jack Mills with his bandage round his head were used to justify our 30-year sentences. Without those images, it would have been almost impossible to sway public opinion against us and give us 30-year sentences for an unarmed robbery where all the staff on the train lay down and did nothing. Even Biggsy got 30 years. All he did was lay on the grass verge with his old train driver watching the robbery, Ronnie never even set foot on the train he was NOT a big player."

Without doubt, Ronnie Biggs's real time of notoriety came after he escaped from Wandsworth Prison in July 1965. Daring, clever or just plain daft, it certainly catapulted Ronnie Biggs into 'Britain's Most Wanted'. My friend Roy Shaw was sewing mailbags next to Ronnie in Wandsworth Prison in 1965 when Ron asked him if he wanted to go over the wall with him. Considering that (according to the penal system) Roy was supposed to be one of the most out-of-control, violent, anti-authority and disruptive men in the prison system, you would've thought he would've jumped at the chance, but Roy obviously saw a logic that Ronnie missed, and if you compare the lives of the two men now, it's obvious that Roy made the right decision in not going. Ronnie eventually escaped with Eric Flowers. Indeed, Roy became a legitimate millionaire businessman and Ronnie stayed on the run for 30 years. His train money has long, long gone.

So Ronnie Biggs now languishes in his cell in Norwich Prison, Norfolk, in the so-called hospital (Healthcare Unit) wing. In addition to his eating, speaking and walking disabilities that have resulted from his many strokes, he also recently contracted the MRSA superbug. The list goes on. But, like it or not, Ronnie has always been a passive, warm-hearted man. There is no longer any benefit to keeping this extremely sick 79-year-old stroke victim in a high-security prison. They obviously think Biggsy is still an escape risk! Don't forget, this man never even hurt anyone when he was supposedly active 40-odd years ago, so I hardly think he's going to start now, do you?

A lot of good people think that Ronnie should've stayed in Brazil, and I agree with them. Look what he came back to: Hellmarsh (Belmarsh) hospital wing! It has been said that Biggsy was tricked, sold out for money, betrayed and lied to. All I know is, I would rather live out my days in sunny Rio than Belmarsh high-security nick.

On the plus side, Biggsy has some great friends and supporters - not just his pals from the rascal days, such as Bruce Reynolds and Roy Shaw, but straight men like Mike Gray who is an absolute diamond. Ronnie also has overwhelming support from the general public. It's funny that during election times politicians rant on about what the people want, democracy and serving the public, but when it comes to that same public speaking out about injustice it's not the people's business anymore and public opinion counts for nothing. Still, what do you expect?

I would strongly urge the public to show their support for Ronnie. If you feel what's happening is wrong please, please drop Biggsy a line at: PRISONER RONALD ARTHUR BIGGS, 002731, HEALTHCARE UNIT, KNOX ROAD, NORWICH, NORFOLK. People who are absolutely impossible to dislike are very rare, but Ronnie Biggs is one of them, together with Howard Marks, Ronnie Knight and, despite the inaccurate press he gets, Charlie Richardson. With Charlie, the image and the real man couldn't be more different and anyone who actually knows him will tell you that. The same goes for Biggsy and Howard, who are completely lovable rogues.

It's also crucial to remember that if Biggsy was the big, bad criminal he was supposed to be he would've got in trouble in Brazil. After all, the man

- once again contrary to popular belief - was skint. His train money was mostly conned out of him while on the run 40 years ago. In all the years he spent in Brazil he never got in trouble with the law. A criminal with no money usually goes back to crime, but Ronnie Biggs went back to his real trade as a carpenter. Ronnie was really just a rascal, but unlike most rascals he got himself mixed up in a big robbery, a robbery in which he was totally out of his depth. In Britain, men like Freddie Foreman, The Krays, Roy Shaw, Micky McAvoy, Bruce Reynolds, John Knight, Mad Frankie Fraser and Vic Dark were all at one time or another first-class, premier league villains. Ronnie Biggs was NEVER in that class. Nevertheless, on visits to outside hospitals, the authorities still thought it crucial to handcuff him to the bed!

So here's a pensioner, who has had untold strokes, is wired and tubed up, can't talk, has no money and probably didn't know where the hell he was anyway. What did they think he was going to do? Escape? Assault hospital and prison staff? It would be funny if wasn't so tragic. I was reading the newspaper not long ago (Monday, 12 December 2005) and one headline read: "Sick paedo freed for two-day trip. No cuffs for beast on £1,000 journey". It went on: "A sex beast believed to have targeted hundreds of kids was allowed out of Broadmoor WITHOUT handcuffs". So before some of you (because there's always a few) wonder why I and others have so much sympathy for Ronnie Biggs and wonder why we are disgusted that he was handcuffed to a bed whilst ill, read the above, and if you still can't see anything wrong you have serious problems!

Just before Christmas 2002, Ronnie was actually dragged from his bed and given a kicking by two screws. How very brave! Obviously nothing happened to them. It would seem that Ronnie Biggs is being made an example of. But anyone with an ounce of sense will tell you that making an example of Ronnie will NOT deter anyone from crime. It will do no good at all. It will not make anyone have more respect for the law and is in fact causing a backlash against the powers that be because people can see it's inhumane and only cowards and bullies pick on easy targets to make their points!

Biggsy was also kidnapped, with the intention of handing him over to the police, by some big sack of useless shit called John Miller in 1981. To kidnap a man and take him away from his young child with the intention of grassing him up to the police in the name of money is revolting! It is also alleged that a successful comedian put up the money to have Ronnie kidnapped, What a slag! A very well-known boxer was also said to have tried to get Ronnie recaptured by staging a fight show on a ship. The ship would then sail just into British waters and Ronnie would be arrested! It just goes to show that some public figures that people look up to are not what they seem. Funny that they never mention their brave, bold attempts to serve justice in their own memoirs. I was warned very sternly by certain officials that I couldn't mention the comedian's and the boxer's (who was shit by the way) alleged involvement ... Whoops, I just have!

This guy Miller was on a television programme about Ronnie recently and he claimed that he had done Ronnie a favour because the kidnap had made him more famous and he couldn't understand what Biggsy was complaining about! Erm, yeah! The fact that brave Miller said to Ronnie while he was tied up, "The slightest struggle and you're done for", makes a mockery of Miller's claims that it was all cosy and he was actually doing Ron a favour! Miller, you're a cowardly sack of shit and your death will be celebrated by us all! The makers of the programme called *Ronnie Biggs - The Last Escape* had contacted me because they wanted Roy Shaw on the show but didn't know how to get hold of him. I phoned Roy and he agreed to do it. On the show, Roy is filmed suited and booted in a boxing ring, and he speaks well about his days with Biggsy in Wandsworth sewing mailbags. Despite having to point out letters on a chart, Ronnie still speaks about those days and his memory is perfect.

Of course, there are those who maintain that Ronnie Biggs should be punished, but my response is that the unarmed robbery took place over 40 years ago, and his quality of life is so poor that just being awake is painful punishment enough for him. It's not as though he'd be able to swan off on a world cruise and live the high life if he were released, is it? He's a very, very ill 79-year-old man whose suffering will continue.

It's also important to compare Ronnie's circumstances with the crimes committed by others. For instance, in 1967 John McVicar escaped from Durham Prison (which was supposed to be escape-proof), where he was on E wing, a special unit for the most dangerous prisoners. He pulled off another armed robbery while still on the run, shooting a guard in the leg with a shotgun in the process. He was eventually recaptured and sentenced to 26 years, but was released on parole in 1978. How can that be? Don't get me wrong, good luck to John for getting out, but when you compare that to Ronnie Biggs who is still in HMP Norwich, something's not right somewhere. John McVicar's case is only one example of many that I could fill up this book with, but John is one of the more famous ones. He published his memoirs and a film entitled *McVicar* was made about him, starring Roger Daltrey. Once again, good luck to him, but he didn't disappear into anonymity after he came out, which is what the authorities like people to do.

Talking of John McVicar, he does have a tendency to say nasty things about other people and forget he was in fact a villain himself. One particular comment he made that sticks in my mind happened at Ronnie Kray's funeral. He was on the news outside St Matthew's Church and they asked him about the funeral. John replied: "Great funeral, shame about the life." Now I'd say that's pretty judgemental and self-righteous by anyone's standards. He could have carried a lot of respect from the elite of the 'Chaps', but has lost it all by saying such things. It's not necessary and it doesn't make sense when an ex-armed robber is more critical of the underworld than anyone else.

Here are some more examples that highlight the injustice of Ronnie's sentence. Recently Mehmet Ali Agca was released after a 25-year sentence for shooting Pope John Paul II. Can anyone explain how you get 25 years for blasting the Pope with a gun in a packed place and 30 for an unarmed robbery on a train full of banknotes destined to be incinerated? Okay, it's a different country, but the fact is you can't compare those two crimes whatever country you're in. Then, on 2 February 2006, two scum were sentenced for robbing their frail old gran of her life savings, beating the life out of her and then strangling her. After this, they went out for a kebab to 'celebrate'! And what sentence did they receive? Nine years! And, with parole, we're talking about five years. Also not long ago two scum raped an 18-month-old baby and got a paltry six years! They'll probably be out in three. How can you compare that sentence to life imprisonment for non-killers like Ronnie Biggs? How is he more dangerous? Why is everyone so determined to demonise Ronnie Biggs when crimes from hell like this are going on? Please, let's get justice into perspective.

If anyone thinks I'm moaning on too much about these men, please tell me if you think those sentences are perfectly in order. Convince me there's nothing wrong in the gross sentencing inconsistencies for the most heinous of crimes. Men have always and will always rob for money from huge corporate machines, especially men born from roots where daddy can't buy them a fart let alone a Ferrari. You can see why it happens, whether you think it's wrong or not, but raping a baby? Surely it doesn't get any more hellish than that? Do you have any idea what either I, or what I call 'proper' people, would do like to do one of those scum? Still, if we did do anything we'd get arrested and jailed for assaulting THEM!

Nonces have no place on this earth and anyone who sympathises with them is as good as a nonce themselves. I honestly think that every self-respecting citizen should be allowed by law to attack known nonces on sight and be rewarded. The amazing thing is, I just know there's going to be twats reading that statement and saying, "Who does he think he is? He has no right." Fuck off! Nonces are there to be hurt, and if you don't have the decency to do it or ring someone that will do it, may you burn in hell!

Some may say quite simply that a criminal is a criminal, but it doesn't take much to work out that that's rubbish. Ronnie Biggs is NOT the same as Ian Brady; 'Razor' Smith is NOT the same as Ian Huntley; and Kenny Noye is NOT the same as Dennis Nielsen. Abul Hamza was found guilty of conspiracy to murder and instructing his followers to kill non-Muslims. He was also labelled Al Qaeda's main man in Europe. And he received nine years! That means that Ronnie Biggs is considered more dangerous than men who preach hate and violence with known links to Al Qaeda! John Humble, aka the Wearside Twat, sent hoax letters and tapes to George Oldfield during the hunt for the Yorkshire Ripper. The police diverted their hunt to the Sunderland area, only considering suspects with a north-east accent, and during that time Peter Sutcliffe killed three more innocent women. On arresting Sutcliffe, the Old Bill even queried whether he had a north-east accent. Humble thought it a laugh to divert the police while Sutcliffe slaughtered the women, but the Wearside Twat drew just eight years! Can anybody actually justify that?   To me, Ronnie Biggs's sentence is all about class. The class system is alive and well, thank you very much, and it has a long memory.

So what will become of Ronnie Biggs? My guess is that the authorities will not have the courage to release him. Ronnie is too popular and has too many supporters for them to do that. That lesson was learned when supporters campaigned for the release of Reg Kray. That alone should give everyone a cause for concern. It would seem that, in a so-called democracy, having support and a public consensus of "This is wrong", with thousands of good people willing to stand up for the injustice of your case, is actually a sure-fire way to ensure that you are not released. Work that one out. If nobody supported you and everyone just wanted to forget you ever existed, you would probably be okay. Men in power have always been scared of a show of popularity that is not for them. Because Ronnie is actually a charming, good man and many people like him and see him as a folk hero, this will actually work against him. Equally, if Reg Kray were not as popular with the man in the street he would probably have seen

11

freedom years ago. Reg should have been released when his sentence was up but he wasn't. The difference between Reg and Biggsy is that Reg did actually kill someone, whereas Ronnie didn't, although in this bizarre system it would probably have turned out better for him if he had done.

It's easy to put those who support certain people in prison in some sort of pigeonhole, label them with some sort of mental, psychological or social problem and dismiss them. The truth, as always, is different. Most supporters are intelligent and have children, and if you have children you're simply not going to want men or women who may put them in danger on the streets, so a great deal of conviction, thought and sense of injustice goes into it. There simply cannot be a single person who knows all their facts that can possibly think Ronnie Biggs is dangerous.

Roy Shaw, Mike Gray and myself will be visiting Ronnie Biggs again in a couple of weeks' time. We will pass on messages of respect from all the 'Chaps' like we usually do. How Ronnie responds to these messages depends on the day. I honestly fear for a society in which punishment is ruled by vindictive revenge and rehabilitation is kicked into touch with heartless passion just to show who's boss. You have to worry about a society that makes you wonder if you would have been treated less harshly if you had killed someone! Ronnie still has the will to live - just.

Let's just recap on the facts here. The Great Train Robbery in which Ronnie Biggs played a very minor role took place 45 years ago! Ronnie is now an extremely sick 79-year-old man. He is still in maximum security. Can anyone REALLY justify this?

God bless you Ronnie, mate, and see you soon. Tel Currie.

Chapter 2
The Curse of the Train Robbers

(by Tel Currie)

*"Too many people knew about this bit of work and it
was going to end in tears." - Freddie Foreman*

Time has not been kind to the Great Train Robbers. In fact, like those who
discovered Tutankhamun's burial site at the start of the last century, many
believe that the Great Train Robbery was cursed. I personally don't believe
this theory, because surely the chief of the Tutankhamun adventure,
Howard Carter, and the mastermind behind the train robbery, Bruce
Reynolds, would have been the first to suffer the horrific curse. This never
happened, of course, and in fact Bruce is still very much alive I'm a pleased
to say. As for Howard Carter, he died of natural causes many years later.
However, what cannot be ignored is the fact that both adventures ended
with many questions still unanswered.

Out of the other Train Robbery gang members, Charlie Wilson was of
course assassinated at his villa in Spain in 1990, Roy James died on the
operating table during a somewhat experimental heart operation, Brian
Field was killed in a car accident and Bobby Welch had serious walking
difficulties for some years. Bill Boal had in fact had absolutely nothing to
do with the Train Robbery but was sentenced anyway in what must be one
of the greatest miscarriages of justice in British legal history, and Tommy
Wisbey was sentenced along with Eddie Richardson on a cocaine charge
(both Tommy and Eddie are now free). One of the three Train Robbers

who got away and was never charged and who was a very close friend of Bruce Reynolds has also passed away.

Bruce Reynolds's health hasn't been great for a while now either, although I'm pleased to say I spoke to Bruce a couple of weeks ago and he's remaining positive. We had a good chat about which people we rated and which ones we didn't and we had a bit of a heart to heart. I have the ultimate respect for Bruce. I would say that, among the Chaps, Bruce and Charlie Richardson are the most intelligent, most highly read men I have met. There's always a book that they insist you must read. Charlie has given me a load of books lately, including ones on evolution, science and motor racing and one called *Honour Thy Father*, which is about 600 pages long. You name it and Charlie and Bruce have read it.

Of course, Buster Edwards' suicide shocked everyone. What also seemed shocking was that Frankie Fraser fell out with Buster because, according to Frank, he had met Buster when he was on his way to give evidence for the prosecution in the trial of the Taylor sisters. I have to say, however, that I've never heard this from anyone except Frank. Charlie Wilson's murder was also a real shocker, and there's something about a suicide that makes everyone think that maybe, just maybe, they could've said or done something to prevent the tragedy.

In Buster's case, what makes the matter worse is the fact that Busters despair seems to point more and more at one man's stupidity and incompetence ... that, and 30 tons of coffee granules. At this time Buster had lost some merchandise, the council was going to close his beloved flower stall outside Waterloo Station and he was skint. The sale of all that coffee was going to put him something like back on track. The coffee had to be delivered to Liverpool, but the driver tried to save money by not filling the lorry up with diesel and as a result it conked out and he just left it where it was. Buster's lifeline had gone up in smoke. The combination of financial ruin and the possibility of going back to prison was very hard to swallow. The next day Buster hung himself in the lock-up of his flower stall after drinking a bottle of vodka. It was an absolute tragedy. Buster's tragic story also put paid to the view still held by some that the Train Robbers had millions stashed away from 1963. Nothing could be further from the truth.

Another major cock-up occurred in the post-robbery clearing-up process. Someone was simply supposed to go back to the farm that the gang had been using as their base and clean it up after the robbers had left, making sure that all fingerprints were removed and it was completely evidence-free. That never happened, so then it was on to Plan B – burn the place down. Guess what? That never happened either. The bloke never turned up. So there it was - a great big standing clue! And Biggsy's prints were found on a Monopoly board.

This guy must've been one of the worst villains and unluckiest men in general. His name was Tommy Marks, better known as Ginger Marks. In 1965 he was walking down Cheshire Street in Bethnal Green with his mate Jimmy Evans, when he thought somebody called him from a car. Marks bent down to see who was in the car, shots were fired and Marks was never seen again. His disappearance into thin air would later be repeated on Jack McVitie and Frank Mitchell. Marks was not a mistake - he was supposed to get it as well, but Jimmy Evans was target number 1.

In one of life's ironies, the guy who coshed Jack Mills and as a result got most of the others 30 years was one of the three robbers who were never caught! The length of those ridiculous sentences caused outrage among the public and some factions of the law, but the law justified it every time by bringing up the coshing of the driver. Without that, such draconian sentences could never have been dished out. So the fact that the one man that got them those sentences was never caught must have been extremely difficult to accept. However, the Train Robbers were all men of honour and at no time in the 43 years since the robbery has a single one of them revealed the names in public of those who got away or that of the man who coshed the driver. Of course, it's all well known in certain circles,

15

but it has never been made available for public consumption. When you consider the treachery that's gone on with all the other major robberies since, it's amazing that all these men have kept quiet since 1963! I don't think that type of 'wall of silence' would ever happen again, especially with a job of that size. Nowadays people are falling over themselves to grass on others, So unless you have been lucky enough to have been told personally by one of the Train Robbers who was involved, you will never know, not while some are still alive anyway.

The man who had ordered the hit on Charlie Wilson, Roy 'The Lump' Adkins, was gunned down in September 1990 - shot five times in the head. The other two men accused of being involved in the killing of one of the most liked Train Robbers were Danny 'Scarface' Roff and Billy 'Porky' Edwards. Roff was shot in 1996 and suffered a severe spinal injury that confined him to a wheelchair. But Roff did not escape his final punishment. As he parked up his driveway in March 1997, two masked men pulled up and shot him in the head and chest. Surely these men couldn't have been stupid enough to think you can kill a man like Charlie Wilson and get away with it? Billy 'Porky' Edwards is still alive but will have to spend his life on the run. Charlie's old pal Freddie Foreman said chillingly: "These things are never forgotten. It doesn't matter how much time goes by, it will not be forgotten. Payback can come at any time." Coming from a man whose nicknames are 'The Undertaker' and 'Brown Bread Fred', that's rather worrying. But it's pretty obvious that this would be the case. Keep running, Porky!

The Train Robbery also throws up the contrast in opinions between Fred and Frankie Fraser. Fred says: "I was asked to take part in the train robbery but declined. Too many people knew about this bit of work and it was going to end in tears." Frank, on the other hand, insists: "My two big regrets in life are, one, that I was never part of a major robbery and, two, that I never took part in the Great Train Robbery." When you consider what happened to most of the robbers, you would have to agree with

Fred. It's a massive price to pay to be a legend.

As for Ronnie Biggs's plight, was anyone to blame for tempting him back from Brazil? I'm afraid in the underworld names get thrown up just because the one saying them has a longstanding grudge with the other. If I had a pound for every time I heard the word 'grass' being hurled about. Of course, names have been thrown up and I have had doubts, but the fact is that Ronnie was extremely ill back then and still is today (2008). He was simply too ill to stay in Brazil and wanted to die in his homeland. He was promised a financial deal from a top newspaper that would have solved all his solvable problems. It didn't. It got swallowed up by legal and medical bills, and Ronnie was arrested on the plane at RAF Northolt, England.

So the Great Train Robbery has long been and gone, and as I write (August 2008) Ronald Arthur Biggs is still here and still stuck in HMP Norwich. Norfolk.

Chapter 3
It all Began in the
Summer of '65
(by Mike Gray)

I grew up as a prison officer's son and Wandsworth Prison in south-west London, which opened in November 1851 as The Surrey House of Correction, was my childhood neighbour. From 1878 to 1961 it was the scene of 135 hangings, mainly for the crime of murder, but also for spying during the wars and for treason. Fortunately, conditions have improved vastly since those days, although while I was a child there always seemed to be something kicking off there and this particular day was no exception.

It was 8 July 1965, I was nine years old, and I was playing football on the prison officers' quarters' football pitch with my friends, who were all prison officers' sons. Suddenly, around 3 p.m. on this very sunny summer's afternoon the prison siren began to sound, which signalled an attempted or successful escape. It continued for a long time, and we then saw prison officers actually coming out of their houses and others running around in a sort of frenzy. We all ran round the corner past the old Turrett housing, which lay on each corner of the Wandsworth Prison, and as we ran the two minutes or so we could see a large crowd gathering only about 200 yards away.

I could see a large red furniture van parked close up to the prison wall. Prison officers were turning up in numbers, some wearing the summer white jackets and others the more familiar navy uniforms. Police cars were arriving, with the bell on the roof ringing out and the blue lights on the front grill flashing. I first thought someone must be on the floor surrounded by all these people, as me and my friends were told to keep away, move further back, go back to the playing field. These instructions became louder as a police officer started shouting through a megaphone, and the surge of people pushed us further away.

The red furniture van was now being inspected from every angle, and I could see police and prison officers climbing onto its roof and then onto the prison wall. Television camera crews were arriving and setting up their equipment. One of my mates then told me that our other pal had been locked in the coal shed next to his house and that his mother had seen everything that had happened and the TV people were filming her and we would all see her on TV that night. It all seemed hard to believe, but we soon discovered via our own parents and other adults that a high-profile criminal had got over the prison wall via a rope ladder, jumped into the back of the furniture van, which was covered in mattresses to break the fall, and then hopped into a waiting car, which drove off into Heathfield Road and vanished.

As everyone was milling around the prison wall and the red furniture van, I heard a name mentioned for the very first time, and, although it meant absolutely nothing to me at that point, it would become part of my everyday life about eight years further down the line. The name I heard was Ronald Biggs, a train robber. I didn't even know what a train robber was, let alone anything about Ronald Biggs. Oh well, life as a nine-year-old goes on. I did watch the black-and-white news that night and saw Mrs Williams, who claimed she'd seen everything through her prefab house kitchen window. She also confirmed that her son had been locked in the coal shed by the getaway drivers, who later on in history were identified as Paul Seabourne and his mate.

At Wandsworth Prison something was always happening: prisoners climbing onto the prison roof and throwing slates down; prisoners wanting to commit suicide being talked off the roof; fires breaking out, with black smoke pouring over the walls. Some prisoners once tried to jump into the back of the rubbish truck as it made its way through the main gates, and on another occasion a bulldozer was used to ram the wall of the laundry, which had a separate entrance to the prison only about 100 yards from were the red furniture van was parked, and several inmates escaped and made their way behind the row of prefab housing and down onto the railway bank, which backed onto Earlsfield Road.

The prison officers' quarters were separated from the main public road by horseshoe-shaped Heathfield Square, which bordered each side of the prison walls and was lined with houses. Behind the prison lay Strickland Row, comprising blocks of terraced housing, with small concrete backyards, and also the Prison Officers' Social Club, which had a large lounge, a snooker room with two tables and a large dance hall with a hatch through to the bar.

'The Club', as it was known, looked out onto the full-sized football pitch and a sand pit. Every year the pitch was used for the prison sports day, held for officers' children aged 10 to 14, with winners being awarded trophies, etc. The football pitch was cut and marked out by inmates, as in those days they had day duties, and they also decorated our flats and houses. Another yearly event was the bonfire, which was erected on the centre of the football pitch. It was always a massive bastard and it meant that the centre circle would completely burn and for days after the smouldering ash would prevent football matches taking place.

In later years the prison officers entered a local football league - Morden and District, and the original name of the team was eventually changed from Wandsworth Prison Officers to Heathfield Rangers due to the number of incidents on the pitch and numerous players being sent off. This was all rather stupid I thought. I was 14 years old and, along with four of my mates (all officers' sons), I was playing with the adults for Wandsworth Prison Officers football team. When the name was changed it obviously didn't take long for other teams in our division to realise that we were the old Wandsworth Prison Officers team, seeing as the address we gave for our home games was Groom Crescent, just behind the prison!

The father of one of my mates in that team got a mention in Ronnie Biggs's first book. He was the screw who used to sit outside Ronnie's cell when he was reviewing his 30 years in Wandsworth, and Ronnie used to say that he would fidget on his wooden chair, making it creak throughout the evening, and he would then hear the rustle of foil as he opened his sandwiches and the sound his flask being opened, as well as the usual bodily functions of burping and farting.

Nine Years Later ...

1974 saw me looking for vacancies in the journalistic world, as I had my heart set on being a reporter for a national newspaper. I was in the process of taking my English O level at Spencer Park Comprehensive, Wandsworth, and one part of the exam required the pupils to watch *News at Ten* on the evening of Friday 2 February, take any one of the main featured stories and spend the whole weekend researching, interviewing and locating documents/photographs and anything else we could find that was related to that particular story. The completed assignment had to be presented at 9 a.m. the following Monday to the tutor, who would also have watched the news so that he could verify the subjects we had chosen. This was all part of being a potential journalist - being sent to investigate a story, being as thorough as possible, and producing a well-researched article within a certain time frame. I was very much into scrapbooks and writing, so I couldn't wait for this opportunity and, of course, the bonus of passing my English O level, which would be essential for gaining employment in this field.

I could hardly wait for the start of *News at Ten* that evening, and was transfixed as the newsreader, Andrew Gardner, chimed out the first story: "Great Train Robber Ronald Biggs has been rearrested in Brazil after nine years on the run". Dong - another story was announced, and then another, but I had heard that name again - the one that I had first heard on 8 July 1965 - Ronald Biggs. My mind was already made up. After all, I'd had

21

personal experience of the subject already, as I'd only been 200 yards from where he had escaped in 1965. I was sure that the TV crews and press would now revisit the scene of the escape, so I would be able to gather first-hand information from actual journalists and reporters and the papers would be full of stories and photographs of Ronald Biggs. Yes, I knew that some of the other students might take this as their subject as well, but I had that all-important edge - I was there. I could remember the dodgy red furniture van, my mate had been locked in the coal shed by the getaway drivers, and his mother (who still lived in the same house) had witnessed Biggs's escape. I had everything I needed. By the end of that evening, I had already scribbled down lots of notes, recalling as many details as possible. Not surprisingly, this was followed by a restless night's sleep as I eagerly awaited the break of dawn and the commencement of the Ronald Biggs project.

The following morning I bought every newspaper that made the slightest mention of Ronald Biggs from Johnson's Newsagents in Trinity Road, opposite the County Arms pub, where I used to work between 5 and 8 a.m. My job involved untying the bundles of papers and marking them up for the paper boys, who on Saturdays tended to come in earlier than usual as it was pay day, and then sorting the papers for the shop counters, as there were always early birds looking to buy a newspaper, even on a cold February morning such as that. I also had to bundle up the quota for Wandsworth Prison, which I loaded onto a porter's trolley, together with any magazines ordered, and had to deliver to the prison gate by 7 a.m. Those first two hours of the morning were always very busy, especially on Sundays due to the onset of a supplements trend – The Times was massive enough on its own without all those! After the 'prison run', as we called it, I would hang on from 7 till 8 a.m. just to make sure that none of the paper boys failed to turn up for their rounds, although on pay day that was would be unusual.

As I read through all the newspapers, I digested every word and photograph - especially the 1965 escape photos - and kept saying to myself: "Was I really standing right there?" Headlines jumped out from every paper: "They've Got Him ... Biggs Recaptured ... Arrested After 9 Years on the Run", etc. As events unfolded and negotiations were conducted on the other side of the world over the following 24 hours, the headlines kept changing, but normal weekend life continued for me. As well as my work at the newsagents I had a Saturday job, as we all did at the time, in the Woolworths store at Clapham Junction - on the dog food counter, of all places! We had to wear brown coats like you see on *Grace Brothers*, while on the shop floor, but the pay was decent and it gave me the cash to buy the seven-inch vinyl 'Trojan sound' reggae records that I had loved since 1969. Clapham Junction had a good selection of shops selling this type of music, such as Slipped Disc and Reading's in Lavender Hill or John's record stall in Clapham Junction Market next to the Windsor Castle pub - happy days.

Monday morning came and my tutor saved the best till last - the class's projects. As it happened, only two of the other pupils had chosen the Ronnie Biggs story as their subject, and I thought their work was a pretty poor effort if they wanted to be reporters. My project stood almost a foot high: cuttings stuck into numerous scrapbooks; notes I had written; and diagrams of the prison around which my life had revolved, having been born in Lambeth, South London, in June 1957. I received a commendation from the school head and my tutor, and I remember my tutor saying to me, "Here's your project, Mike. Keep it going. It could make you famous one day."

Famous? I thought. I don't think so. But I took it home and kept the cuttings going, buying at least one of the main newspapers every day, especially if the front-page headlines featured Ronald Biggs. Let's face it, from his rearrest in February through to Michael Biggs being born in August, Ronnie was never off the front page. So the collecting continued from 1974 onwards, and by the time 1989 arrived my collection was so vast that it filled a large adult suitcase. It was then that I decided I wanted to take it one step further, my tutor's words 15 years earlier echoing in my ears.

There was a London newspaper called *Loot*, which was circulated in almost every city in the world, such was its success, so I decided that I would place a free ten-liner in the Rio De Janeiro edition of the Brazilian *Loot* newspaper in August 1989. As we didn't have e-mail back then and I wasn't prepared to give out my home phone number either, I simply said, "Ronnie Biggs press cuttings wanted. Will send your wants from UK", followed by my address, etc. The advert was faxed to the London office, which then sent it on to the Rio branch. A few weeks passed and not a single letter arrived. Then, in early September, an airmail letter arrived from a young fellow in Rio de Janeiro who was a collector of Beatles memorabilia, and he explained that their material was very hard to find/buy in South America. He had listed several Thomas the Tank Engine cassettes that he wanted (which feature Ringo Starr, the Beatles' drummer, as narrator) and in return he said he would send press cuttings from Rio. Having worked in Woolworths, I knew that the store sold book/cassette packs for 25 pence each. Result, I thought. So I bought four different tapes, packaged them up and off they went to Brazil via airmail.

After a wait of around two weeks, I thought I had been ripped off, but it had only cost me £1 and I was earning £12 at Woolies, so it wasn't going to skint me out. However, a very familiar airmail letter dropped through my door, postmarked Brazil. I opened the letter and read the reply from 'The Thomas collector':

"Mike, I cannot thank you enough for the four tapes you sent. They were out of this world. I know I am being cheeky, but I am now asking you for the other four to make up the set. But as a thank you I am not enclosing press cuttings from here in Rio about Senor Biggs, I am enclosing his home phone number and house address - I look forward to receiving the other tapes. Your friend Eduardo, Rio, Brazil."

I had to think over this letter for a few days. Was it a wind-up? But why should it be? Might it be one of Eduardo's pals pretending to be Ronnie? No, because I have heard his TV interviews and I know the sound of his voice. After almost a week of deliberations, on 18 September 1989 I said to my wife, "I'm going to call this number," fortunately remembering that Rio was ten hours ahead of the UK, and so I began to dial …

"Ronnie, it's Mike Gray from London." Worrying about Ronnie's reply was what had taken me so long to make the call. However, it became obvious that Eduardo had covered his back and had confirmed with Ronnie that I could contact him, when I heard Ronnie reply, "What took you so long?" Ronnie told me that he had known Eduardo for years and he was studying English at the university in Rio, etc., so I needn't have worried for a week before finally taking that step to speak to the man himself. I then wrote to Ronnie in Sepetiba, a very quiet fishing village, as he wasn't living in Santa Theresa then. That's why the UK press found it difficult to locate him for any exclusives.

One of the things that Ronnie said he couldn't get for love nor money in Brazil was the very hard liquorice that he had loved since his childhood. No one in Rio had heard of it and his UK visitors only sent or took him the soft liquorice. I had started work in Green Park by then and was able to track down a olde worlde confectionary shop in Piccadilly, central London, so I bought Ronnie loads of the stuff, wrapped it up and mailed it to him. In October 1989, a month after first contacting Ronnie, he wrote to say that the liquorice had arrived. As a gesture of thanks, Ronnie sent me photographs with his signature, messages, lyrics, you name it. Obviously I couldn't send him cash, as it was illegal in Brazil for him to receive it, so goods became the currency. Whatever Ronnie wanted, I posted it to him. Our friendship had started and my next planned step was to meet him face to face.

I had told many of my friends about my contact with the UK's most wanted man. Even though he was safe in Brazil, he was still the subject of a possible extradition order from the UK Government. In 1997, the Home Office sent a notification to the Brazilian authorities that they were no longer interested in Mr Biggs and he could stay a free man so long as he didn't leave Brazil. But my contact with Ronnie soon brought an unexpected and worrying twist.

My home phone rang late one night. "Mr Gray, don't speak just listen," said a voice in a very matter-of-fact way. The background noise sounded like a club or pub. He continued, "We know your package got through to Mr Biggs and we will expect you to send more, but for us. You will not open them, just post them as normal. Do you understand? We will be in touch." The phone went dead.

Fuck me, I thought. What have I done? All this eagerness to contact the UK's most wanted criminal has placed me in a very serious position. Why did I want to do it? Why did I go ahead with it? Couldn't I have just have been happy collecting press cuttings? Oh my God ...

I went into the lounge and my wife, Lita, asked who was on the phone. All I could say in reply was, "What have I done?" She noticed straight away that I had turned white and was looking very worried. I just kept on repeating, "What have I done? ... Why did I do it?" To a certain degree I was actually cursing Ronnie Biggs for becoming part of my everyday life.

Noticing how much anxiety the phone call had caused, Lita realised that she couldn't let me suffer any longer and said to me, "Mike, it's a wind-up, the man telling you about the packages ..."

Well, I was ecstatic with relief on first hearing her words, but I then felt incredibly angry that she knew it was a wind-up.

Lita's response was: "Let that be a lesson to you. You must be very careful about who you are contacting and why, and who you share certain information with."

I now realise that these were very wise words. I found out that the person behind the wind-up was my brother-in-law, Brian Riordan, who worked in the legal profession. He had got a pal of his to call me from a

London boozer and Lita knew all about it. It was a harsh lesson learnt, but I respect Brian and Lita for it. I love you both.

I continued with my weekly phone calls and letters to Ronnie throughout the 1990s, and my press cuttings were soon in danger of overflowing into a second large suitcase. Michael Biggs e-mailed me in 1999 to say that Ronnie had requested my company at his 70th birthday party in Rio, and I was advised to speak with Nick Reynolds about catching the same flight as him, together with his father Bruce Reynolds, Roy (Prettyboy) Shaw, Tony Hoare and Dave Courtney. Unfortunately, I had a family holiday booked for that date in August, and not finding a cheap flight to Rio via Paris and attending that function is something I will always regret. Not long after the party Ronnie had another, much more serious stroke – one that stopped him from speaking and paralysed him down one side. Such is life.

I still look back to 1988, when I came across (not literally!) a copy of the adult magazine *Men Only*, published by Paul Raymond (aka The King of Soho). Inside was Part Two of 'The Ronnie Biggs Interview'. Paul Raymond and his younger daughter Debbie were in Rio de Janeiro and did an exclusive interview with Ronnie. It contained some superb photographs of him and Mr Raymond, together with his attractive daughter, the most famous one being that of Ronnie on Corcovado mountain in Rio, standing in front of the Statue of Christ. Other photos included Ronnie on a moped with Debbie.

It was frustrating that Part Two of the interview had been published a year or so before I found it, and it was impossible to track down a back copy of the *Men Only* issue featuring Part One. However, I wrote to Mr Raymond and explained about My Biggsy collection, etc., and told him about my quest to find a back copy of that specific magazine issue, and after a few weeks I received a photocopy of the article from Debbie Raymond herself. She apologised for not being able to send out an original, but the office's archive only contained that one original issue. I called her and thanked her so much. We had a long chat about her meeting with Ronnie in Brazil and she told me how she'd found him to be a really nice person and that she and her father had enjoyed his company over the week they were with him. In the late '80s and early '90s Paul Raymond began handing over control of his massive publishing empire to his daughter Debbie, and I was very saddened to hear that Debbie had passed away in 1992. Paul Raymond also passed away earlier this year (2008). I will always remember her and the Ronnie Biggs connection.

Michael told me that he and his father were setting up the Ronnie Biggs website and they wanted me to be part of their limited company, called The Biggs Experience. I was given the title of Media Researcher and Michael and Ronnie arranged for business cards to be printed to confirm the position, which detailed Ronnie's home phone number and address. Other members of the board of directors were Nick Reynolds, Brian Running and Giovanni (Brazilian Gio, not Italian) and Jamal (Jim) Shreim. I sent Ronnie and Michael a stack of my UK press cuttings, which they used on the website as illustrations on all the pages. There was a 'Contact Us' section, and Ronnie actually went live on a daily basis, mailing people with answers to questions or just sending positive messages. On the first day of going live we had thousands of hits on the website, but due to the rapid deterioration of Ronnie's health it was the end as quickly as it had been the beginning. The website needed funds and plenty of time spending on it, so as a result it was not as proactive as it was at first, and now Ronnie wanted to come home.

Michael called me to ask a massive favour. He wanted me to try to find an MP who might possibly represent Ronnie in the Houses of Parliament should he return to the UK. I managed to seek out Harry Cohen MP, a well-established Labour MP for the Leyton and Wanstead constituency who was active both locally and internationally, and got Michael to link up with him to see if he could and would be able to help with Ronnie's legalities should he return to the UK.

It was now late April 2001, and the e-mails and phone calls between me and Michael were few and far between. I knew that he was not at his father's house, as he had told me that they were hiding from the UK media due to a *Sun* newspaper deal, and fair play to him. Even under those circumstances, however, he still called me to keep me updated, and I feel very honoured that he did so. On the evening of 5 May he called to say:

"It's Mike. We (Ronnie included) are on the way to the airport, and the *Sun* newspaper is announcing it on the front page in the morning. I will call you when we are in the UK. Take care, love to the family man. All the best …"

On 6 May the *Sun* newspaper's front page said it all: "Biggs Back".

The rest of my story is a continuing history, with regular prison visits to see Ronnie. Maybe, as a result of this book, my tutor from February 1974 will be proved right - my Ronnie Biggs connection could one day make me famous.

Chapter 4
Welcome to Hellmarsh
(by Mike Gray)

With Ronnie's return to high security in May 2001, the media scramble for a visit to see him was soon under way. Every Tom, Dick and Harry wanted to stake a claim for a visit, with such one-liners as: "I knew Ronnie in Rio some 17 years ago ... I bought him a drink, he must remember me ... We got well pissed together in Rio ... Oh, the green fields of England"! And the all-time classic: "I would love a pint in a pub in Margate." Blah ... boring. Ronnie all of a sudden became the red tops' (*Sun* and *Mirror*, *News of the World*, *People*, etc.) favourite, although over the years Ronnie has always been great fodder for these papers to sell extra copies. And who says the Ronnie Biggs story is boring? It certainly is not, and it just keeps on running and running, just like the legend himself. As for the Margate line, Ronnie's all-time favourite seaside resort was Brighton. He and the boys plus his wife Charmian would be regular visitors, as it was only 30 minutes from Ronnie's house in Redhill to the coast.

Brighton and Hove was the resort where, in July 1963, Ronnie won a treble bet on the horses and collected a massive return of £500, the exact amount that he and Charmian wanted for a deposit on their house in Alpine Road, Redhill. But the seed was already sown. Ronnie had promised Bruce Reynolds that he was in on the train job and he fully intended to honour that pledge to his old friend. And the rest of the story, as they say, is history.

Michael Biggs was very efficient with his telephone calls and e-mails regarding his father. Michael was a natural at responding to enquiries about his father with very constructive, informative and, most of all, honest answers. One thing you will always get from Michael is honesty. After years of being in front of the media as well as dealing with people on a one-to-one basis, he is calm, confident and a great credit to his father. It has been said before, and it is something that I too have always maintained, that sometimes the mannerisms, the reactions, the answers, the content and his plain, ordinary attitude are one and the same as Ronnie's. They are the same person; Michael is Ronnie and vice versa. Over the years the classic bickering between the two has always ended in a great, somewhat cynical but also humorous, line. Ronnie would say, "Son, you are only Ronnie Biggs's son," to which Michael would reply, "Dad, you are only the father of Michael Biggs." In truth, the fame they share between them is more than any normal person could ever hope to achieve, even in two lifetimes.

Michael was now totally in control of interviews and press calls, whereas in Brazil Ronnie was still shuffling about at home and still had a certain clout. He can throw a strop as well as the next person - sulk, moan, ignore. Oh yes, Biggsy senior is very good at that! However, now that he was inside HMP Belmarsh Michael was left to fend off the wolves knocking at his door, but he handled it very well. We, i.e. all the family and close friends, pledged to help in every way we could, of course, but at the end of the day the UK and world media wanted to speak to one person only, Ronnie's nearest and dearest, the mouthpiece of the legendary Great Train Robber.

Ronnie had yet again become Prisoner 002731, the exact same number he was given in April 1964 when he entered HMP Wandsworth to start his draconian 30-year sentence for a robbery in which the only part he played was sitting in a jeep and watching it all take place. He never even set foot on that locomotive train - the embankment was as far as the other train robbers would let him get. And after the retired engine driver brought in by Ronnie was unable to operate the train, he and Ronnie were very lucky not to have sustained serious injuries from the other robbers, as the old boy's actions almost ruined the train robbery and stopped it dead in its tracks.

I called Michael a few days after Ronnie was locked back up in Belmarsh and asked him how he was doing. He replied that he was exhausted and that he was due to visit his dad on the coming Saturday, but that his visitation rights would be restricted to once a month. Michael and Ronnie had been together almost every day in Brazil, so for him now to be allowed to see him only once every month was harsh, and I wondered if the Home Office had got that wrong. We just had to wait and see. Michael told me that he had seen me on the Sky and BBC news programmes, and he complimented me on the confident way in which I had put across the strong and important message that Ronnie should not be held in the UK's most secure prison and had queried why it had needed 20 police vehicles to meet him at Hendon Airport. Michael also said that my suit and tie made the whole Biggs family seem very intelligent, which we are. I think the press were expecting to see morons in Doc Martens and ripped T-shirts with 'The Gonads' on it or something! That's just typical of the UK press, prejudging everyone, especially Ronnie's family and friends and the supporters of the Ronnie Biggs campaign.

I was not used to the press and TV attention prior to Ronnie's return. A story with photograph in the local press would've sufficed back then, but this time it was almost like having a Hollywood set installed on my suburban doorstep, with a Sky TV juggernaut setting up for a live interview and other lorries and vans quickly taking its place when it left. At one point, when Ronnie was in mid-air and scheduled to land in the UK on the Saturday morning, on the Friday night I had a BBC live 24-hour news crew in my front lounge, an ITN world broadcast in my rear lounge, and the phone was ringing non-stop with calls from other media groups, such as BBC Radio London, GLR, etc. It was absolutely crazy! However, I must admit I enjoyed every single minute of it, and I did it all for Ronnie Biggs, as I am still doing today - 2008.

On Saturday 6 May, Ronnie landed at Hendon and I was picked up in a chauffeur-driven Mercedes and driven to the BBC studios for a live interview. I actually took my father-in-law Tommy Thornton with me, who is the same age as Ronnie, as he was loving the occasion as much as I was. He had spoken to Ronnie on the phone whilst at a previous New Year's Eve party held at our home. I had called Ronnie to wish him a happy New Year, and so Tommy had a few words with him too. The BBC interview was full of awkward questions regarding Ronnie, but I handled it with confidence and honesty. I wore a different suit and tie to the previous occasion and once again was given some strange looks over my attire on arriving at the studios.

As Ronnie's first weeks slowly settled into the first month, Michael called me to discuss the visiting arrangements. It went without saying that Bruce and Nick Reynolds would be the first names on the visiting list, as they had both travelled back to the UK with Ronnie on board the Sun Newspapers private jet. I think I was somewhere around fourth in the pecking order for a visit, which wasn't too bad was it? Also on the list was Gus Dudgeon (Elton John's ex-manager, who sadly died in a car accident with his wife Sheila less than a year later); Giovanni, who had travelled back home after living in Brazil; and Jim (Jamal), a neighbour and very close friend of Ronnie's. But to be told that my first visit would be around 30 May, four weeks after Ronnie's return, and also that I would be accompanied by Michael, was great news. Michael, of course, was the first to walk through Belmarsh Prison gates for a visit a week after Ronnie returned, and by all accounts - particularly his own - it was like a fate worse than death.

Belmarsh Prison is a high-security prison in the Thamesmead area of the London borough of Greenwich, in south-east London. It opened on 2 April 1991 and is able to hold up to 915 prisoners. Between 2001 (Ronnie's introduction to Belmarsh) and 2005, the prison was used to detain a number of people indefinitely without charge or trial under the provisions of Part 4 of the Anti-Terrorism, Crime and Security Act 2001, which led to its label as the UK version of Guantanamo Bay. However, a later ruling judged that such imprisonment was discriminatory and against the Human

Rights Act. Belmarsh's short history hasn't passed quietly, with criticisms that health care was inadequate, access to legal advice was restricted, and conditions were cruel, inhumane and degrading. These accusations were made with particular reference to the conditions in which the terror suspects were held - a situation described by David Blunkett as not ideal but necessary - but they applied equally to Ronnie's experiences during his six years there. The prison was built on part of the east site of the former Royal Arsenal Woolwich, adjacent/adjoined to Woolwich Crown Court, which was therefore used for high-profile cases (including those concerning national security). On 4 May 2007, while Ronnie was still at Belmarsh, there was a violent disturbance in the prison, and Sky News reported that at least four prison warders were injured.

Straight after his first visit to his father in May 2001, Michael made a statement to the press and media to quell all the speculation and scaremongering. Was Ronnie being strung up in irons? Was he being fed just bread and water? Was he only permitted to wear a loincloth? Well, these remarks were not far from the truth in a sense, seeing as the prison was supposedly the most modern and secure establishment for housing the UK's most notorious criminals, and Prisoner 002731 was being treated like a child murderer or serial killer. After his nine-hour jet flight to London from Rio de Janeiro, Ronnie was not allowed a bath or shower on his arrival at Belmarsh and did not, in fact, receive permission to do so for more than 48 hours. This was the start of a very long and sad experience for many of us who had never visited a high-security prison before. I, for one, had never set foot in a prison throughout my entire life, let alone one with as much notoriety as HMP Belmarsh.

A very strong supporter of Ronnie's cause, Gus Dudgeon, had known Ronnie and Michael in Rio and he was ever present at our Biggs Amnesty Campaign throughout 2000. We used to meet up at Nick Reynold's studios, called The Tardis, in Clerkenwell, central London, which was also used for many art exhibitions. I remember one such exhibition in particular, entitled 'Cons to Icons', which featured celebrity gangsters such as Ronnie Biggs, Howard Marks, Bruce Reynolds, Roy 'Prettyboy' Shaw, Freddie Foreman, Dave Courtney and others. Nick had sculpted their faces and cast them in bronze. Nick is a very talented young artist and deserves every success he gets - and he's a really nice guy to boot.

The Amnesty Campaign was formed by the board of directors, i.e. me, Nick and Bruce Reynolds, Michael Biggs, Gus Dudgeon and Brian Running, with a view to presenting a scroll to the then home secretary Jack Straw, requesting amnesty on Ronnie's behalf. We conducted meetings as far away from prying press eyes as we could over a period of about nine months, each time discussing when we should make our presentation to Mr Straw. Our unexpected last get-together was early in 2001, as only weeks later Ronnie decided he wanted to come home anyway under his own steam, and therefore the Amnesty Campaign died a very quick death after a somewhat short life. The meetings were always very interesting, however. Mick Gallagher, who used to run the Krays' website, was an ever present, doing anything he could to help the Biggsy cause, and Gus Dudgeon - yes, a multimillionaire but a really down-to-earth fella, God rest his soul - always chipped in with helpful comments about how we could make the Amnesty Campaign work. Thanks for all your support, Gus. Although that particular campaign was over, I assured Ronnie after my first visit that he had lots of close friends just waiting for the chance to go and visit him. I said to him, "Bring on the Belmarsh Boys".

From May 2001 to the end of that year, Ronnie was rushed from Belmarsh on a regular basis to the local Queen Elizabeth Hospital in Woolwich, with stomach ulcers, internal bleeding, suspected stroke, etc. It was almost as though the prison and Home Office couldn't take any chances with him, and so as soon as something wasn't right with Ron, he would be shipped out straight away. In fact on one visit that year, Michael and I turned up at the visitors' centre and were informed in a very unsympathetic and casual manner that Ronnie was not at the prison. To our shock and horror, we were told that Ronnie had been admitted to the QE hospital 24 hours earlier, but no one had bothered to inform his son Michael. Just imagine if something fatal had happened to Ronnie and we'd known nothing about it! That was a close escape, you might assume, but it did happen again.

As the year drew to a close, I compiled a document which I sent to Home Secretary David Blunkett, as well as all the MPs and Home Office officials that I thought might take heed of Ronnie's case and understand the situation as regards the hospital carry-ons. The document was called 'Diary of a Sick Man' and it gave full details of Ronnie's hospital visits. In fact the Diary was used in 2003 as a mail-out with our fund-raising EP's vinyl record sleeves (more about that later) to make the public aware of Ronnie's treatment, and it read as follows:

7 MAY 2001 - *Ronnie returns to UK after suffering two strokes in Brazil.*

3 JUNE 2001 - *Rushed to QE Hospital with suspected third stroke.*

4 JUNE 2001 - *Double cuffed to his hospital bed - I know - I WAS THERE.*

8 JUNE 2001 - *Taken back to HMP Belmarsh from QE Hospital after only five days in hospital.*

12 AUGUST 2001 - *Rushed to QE Hospital - Emergency Blood Transfusion.*

22 SEPTEMBER 2001 - *Rushed to QE Hospital - Internal bleeding and bleeding from back passage.*

2 NOVEMBER 2001 - *Rushed to QE Hospital - Passing blood and continuous vomiting.*

OCTOBER 2002 - *Ronnie banged up for 23 hours a day due to staff shortages in Healthcare Unit.*

OCTOBER 2002 - *Not allowed Association, therefore cannot get anyone to write his Visiting Orders for him.*

NOVEMBER 2002 - *Ronnie diagnosed with skin cancer on his back. He is not treated for two weeks (staff shortages).*

NOVEMBER 2002 - *Not given a bath for two weeks - Again staff shortages* *in Healthcare Unit.*

14 JANUARY 2003 - *Ronnie is assaulted by a member of the prison medical staff.*

I visited with Michael only days after the assault and his stomach had a terrible bruise on it caused by the attack. The story actually makes the *Daily Mail* with the headline of "Biggs Jail assault by Guard".

I visited Ronnie with Michael in September 2001 at Queen Elizabeth Hospital, as rumour had it that he was "knocking on heaven's door". Michael used those very words when he called me, making me realise that this could signal Ronnie's passing. Michael had to call the prison governor to book the hospital visit and give details of the hospital visitors. I had to take along three forms of ID, all with my photo and name on them, which were checked against the Home Office visitors list at the hospital by the two prison officers assigned to Ronnie.

On the day of the hospital visit, the scene around Queen Elizabeth Hospital was chaotic. The press had camped outside the building, causing havoc for all the regular hospital visitors as well as the staff. Ronnie had been allocated a single-occupancy room at the end of B Ward on the first floor, where I was directed once Reception had checked with the prison officers in situ. On arrival, the door was unlocked and I saw that Michael was already in the room with Ronnie and the two prison officers. Ronnie looked gravely ill. I had only seen him eight weeks earlier, but he looked so different now. There he was with tubes coming out of his stomach and nose, and he could barely lift his hand to shake mine. Forget the saying 'Death warmed up', Ronnie was 'Death' full stop. Michael was brushing Ronnie's hair back, and the two officers were sat on the same side of the bed, lunch boxes and flasks on the table. We were able to stay with Ronnie for as long we wanted during the day, but no visits were allowed after 8 p.m. in the evening.

One part of that whole sad scene, however, shocked me more than anything else. "Double-cuffed?" I whispered to myself incredulously. I couldn't believe it. Ronnie had been double-cuffed by his right wrist to the metal hospital bed. When I queried it, one of the prison officers admitted that it was ridiculous, but told me that they were just following orders. I still believe that, if we could've smuggled a photograph of this terrible situation out of that room and given it to the media, a resultant public outcry would've secured his immediate release to a low-security establishment. However, as we were frisked thoroughly, such a plan could never have worked. All Michael could do was cuss and make threats to let the Home Office and UK press know that his seriously ill father - a 71-year-old crippled grandfather - was chained to a hospital bed. Hardly the Yorkshire Ripper, was he? His criminal CV was a total joke.

2002 was as frantic as the end of 2001, with visitors being turned down by the dozen. What some individuals didn't seem to realise was that the decision to accept or decline a visiting order request was not down to Michael or me, it was in Ronnie's hands. In terms of every single visitor and visit, Ronnie only wanted to see who he wanted to see - end of. So if anyone received a visiting order with their name on it, it was pretty special, as it meant that Ronnie had chosen to see them, and getting the nod from the legend to enter the doors of Belmarsh Prison was something only a certain few experienced.

Visitors would first have to report to the Belmarsh Visitors' Centre and then proceed through six security checks once inside the main prison gates. The officers would check every visitor's ID - in the form of a driving licence, passport and utility bill, ensuring that the name and address were the same on each. You then had your hand stamped and your finger inserted (wait for it) into the electronic ID fingering machine (ooohhh, Matron, sounds rather rude!) While this procedure was taking place you also had your mug photographed, and then you had to place your belongings in a locker, only taking into the prison a maximum of £5 per person. No watches, gold chains, or any other items in your pockets (knives, combs, etc.) were permitted. And we hadn't even left the Visitors' Centre yet.

It's a short walk to the main gate entrance, although you don't pass through the main electric gates, as a smaller glass frontage allows you to pass through to a large lobby area. You then queue to enter a small chamber that accommodates about four adults. Once inside, an electric door closes behind you, leaving the rest of the visitors waiting on the other side in the foyer. You then have to insert your finger into a machine again (I've never done so much fingering in a prison!) and the mugshot taken earlier appears after about a minute on a VDU screen. Finally, you hold up your stamped hand and a bright yellow HMP coat of arms is illuminated. These procedures have to be carried out by each of the occupants before another glass door opens electronically to allow everyone to vacate the chamber ready for the next four visitors.

You then find yourself in a search area, where you have to remove your shoes (socks without holes are recommended for visits) and belts and put them in a plastic tray, along with any money, etc. (just as you would if you were heading for the Costa del Crime in Spain and were going through Customs at Gatwick Airport). One by one you are called forward to step through the X-ray facility and into the arms of an awaiting prison officer, who does a manual body search, including your mouth (and don't forget to wiggle that tongue). An X-ray wand is then guided around your body frame just in case the X-ray machine had failed to detect something. Then you can collect your belongings again (better check the money's all there, just in case). You then wait have to wait until the group of security-checked visitors numbers around 12 before another electric steel door opens. As you pass through to the next chamber you see some very large 'Beware of sniffer dogs' warning posters, and again the door slowly grinds shut behind you before another in front of you opens and you are greeted with a very refreshing whiff of fresh air and flowers.

You are now outside and take a one-minute stroll along a gravel pathway to the inner prison. On the right, through the mesh fence, you can see the chapel where Ronnie got married. This leads to another door into a small chamber, which only holds about six adults. The heavy door has to be manually slammed shut and each person goes through the fingering and yellow tattoo routine again. At this point your pass is also checked against the visitor number information displayed on the PC, which has been sent through from the bookings clerk at the Visitors' Centre. It's all very clever but very time consuming, and by the time you sit down with your loved one you've lost quite a bit of your two-hour visiting time. I've always believed that it's all part of the Home Office game, where time is on their side - very interesting if you just stop and think about that one ...

Before releasing you from the final chamber, the officer writes a number on your visiting order. The last time I was in Belmarsh it was no. 27. The chamber leads into the waiting hall, a small reception area with toilets and about 40 seats, where you wait until your number is called out. You have stand in lines of five, spaced two yards behind each other and with your arms down by your sides. The lines are flanked by prison officers, who then instruct the dog handler to let the dog sniff each person in your row, back and front. If, after it has circled you, the dog sits down in front of you, you are removed from the queue and taken to the Inspection Room. If you are caught with anything you shouldn't have, then it's adios to that day's visit, and in some cases the Old Bill will be called in. If nothing is found but the dog senses you're going into overdrive, then you will get a closed visit (i.e. through a glass screen). So if you enjoy a spliff in the comfort of your own home before leaving for Belmarsh or have even had one the night before, then don't wear the same jeans or jacket for the visit, as the little blighters do pick up on the scent. Just be careful.

When you have successfully passed the sniffer test, you can proceed to the glass exit door - yes, I know it sounds boring but, Christ, you should do the visit, it's even worse. Then it's put your hand under the infrared and place your finger in the hole again, before passing your visiting order to one of the three reception/booking officers, who will check you off on their lists and brusquely point you in the right direction to meet your loved one. They've got to know me over the years, but there's never any mention of the name Ronnie or Mr Biggs or just plain Biggs, it's always just "He".

Then you are finally in the visiting hall, equipped with a row of four tables with chairs, all bolted to the floor, located near to the door the inmates use. Three prison officers sit on a raised platform so that they can keep a watchful eye on everyone, and above is a balcony that is also used for surveillance purposes on visits. The Belmarsh visiting hall also has a crèche for the kids and a snack bar run by the League of Friends.

I visited Ronnie three times in HMP Belmarsh (May, July and November) and four times in Queen Elizabeth Hospital throughout 2001. If you were non-family you could only visit every other month at Belmarsh, whereas family members could visit every two weeks initially and this was increased to every week after a year or so. As I mentioned earlier, I joined Michael for my first HMP Belmarsh visit, and it certainly was one to remember. I thought I would show Ronnie respect by dressing in my suit and tie, but this turned out to be a big, big mistake. My tie was confiscated by the search officer and when I entered the visiting hall Ronnie's face on seeing my attire was a picture - he couldn't stop smiling. I looked around the other 62 visitors and there wasn't a suit to be seen - a shell suit or two maybe, but not a quality suit. Ronnie found it very amusing for the full two hours, but worse was to follow …

Ronnie was finding it difficult to spell out words on his A4 laminated sheet, which he still uses today although it was renewed about three years ago, so Michael said, "Dad, write it on the sheet of paper." Ronnie tried to do this, but what he wrote was just a squiggle due to the two strokes he'd suffered. In an attempt to decipher his writing, I took the pencil off Ronnie and tried to copy the letters Ronnie had scribbled. "Hold it!" came a shout from the officers' platform. Then a prison officer approached the three of

41

us, took the pencil from my hand and also removed the sheet of A4 paper. Michael and I just looked at him in shock. "You're not passing on messages," was the officer's response. Even Ronnie looked at us as if to say "Prat". Michael approached the platform in the hall, and requested a very simple explanation. He was told that I was a reporter and they thought I was quizzing Ronnie for a story and he was writing the answers down for me. It seemed totally absurd and pathetic. All Ronnie had to do was point to the A-Z sheet if I wanted any questions answering. But why did they think I was a reporter?

On leaving the visiting hall, a Senior Officer (SO) pulled me aside, which was rather embarrassing in front of all the other exiting visitors. I was informed that they (the prison officers) had assumed I was a reporter because when I had booked into the Visitors' Centre I showed them my employers' pass, which had my photo on in together with my name, home address and signature. At that time I worked in advertising for a publishing company, but the Belmarsh Brains had taken my ID to mean I was a reporter as they had seen the word 'publishing'!

The 'Reporter Saga' has since become a regular talking point during my visits to Ronnie in HMP Norwich, as Ronnie never fails to mention it. It goes without saying that something that has not become a regular feature of my subsequent visits to HMP Belmarsh and Norwich is a suit - I have never worn one on visits since!

I visited Ronnie on 28 November in Belmarsh with Michael, having been informed by Michael that Ronnie had been diagnosed with skin cancer on his back. We discovered that he hadn't received any treatment or seen a skin specialist for a week since the condition had been identified by the healthcare doctor at the prison. Ronnie also said that he had not been allowed a bath for over a week due to staff shortages in the Healthcare Unit. He was told by a senior medical officer, whom he referred to as 'the Dragon', that no care assistants were available to bathe him and so he would have to do strip-wash himself in his cell. Fortunately, his cell had hot water and the radiators were warm, whereas other cellmates weren't so lucky. However, I was appalled that a 73-year-old man who had suffered three strokes and was struggling to walk had been expected to wash himself in this way. After the visit, I telephoned these details through to Mick Gallagher, who ran the Kray twins' website, and he duly posted my findings. As I said to Mick, "It's a fucking liberty and outrageous treatment." I was very grateful to Mick for his support.

Another website that featured Ronnie's plight was Roy (Prettyboy) Shaw's, run by Tel Currie. In 2002 I received an e-mail from Tel Currie, who was very well connected to almost every single underworld character you could mention. Tel had been running the Roy (Prettyboy) Shaw website as well as organising his own boxing tournaments and promotions (Warriors, etc.). I had been in e-mail contact with Tel for many years and he had always shown great and loyal support for Ronnie and Michael Biggs and my attempts to raise awareness of the Biggs cause, whether it be Michael or more importantly Ronnie. Tel used to promote our Biggsy stories on Roy's website, which gave us excellent publicity and kept people informed of Ronnie's up-to-the-minute condition, etc. In his e-mail, Tel said that he and Roy Shaw wanted to visit "the old rascal" - their words, not mine - so I immediately wrote to Ronnie about it. Ronnie hadn't seen his old mate Roy since August 1999, when he had flown to Rio de Janeiro to join Ronnie at his villa for his 70th birthday celebrations, which were actually video-recorded and were later released as a short film called *Father's Day*, produced and directed by Max Carlish - the very man who only a year or so ago tracked down Pete Docherty for a fly-on-the-wall documentary and it all ended up before the beak.

Max had flown to Rio with Bruce Reynolds, Nick Reynolds, Tony Hoare, Dave Courtney and Roy Shaw for Ronnie's birthday bash on 8 August (the same date as the Great Train Robbery), as he was planning to shoot a fly-on-the-wall documentary and also conduct exclusive interviews with these underworld legends. The film is very interesting and also very

43

amusing, as it shows lots of behind-the-scenes footage of Ronnie's party and the camera angles used are superb. At the party, Ronnie's closest old pal Johnny Pickston tells the camera that Ronnie only has 32 glasses and over a hundred people were expected at the part. It shows Ronnie blowing out his candles, with Bruce and Roy in policemen's helmets, and German Frank in the background wondering what the fucking hell was going on! The film also shows Bruce walking around the tiny but picturesque streets of Santa Theresa, a short tram ride away from the vast city of Rio de Janeiro, and also Ronnie on the beach with Bruce Reynolds in his shorts together with Nick and Dave Courtney. Dave was flashing his gold necklaces and sporting his infamous cigar and was attracting the attention of the local Brazilian beauties - superb projection shots.

The camera follows the birthday party through to the next day and features a lot of 'unsung heroes': Giovanni, who was instrumental in helping set up our website and also followed Ronnie back to the UK from Brazil, bringing his young family with him; Jim (Jamal), a really lovely guy, ever present around Ronnie and Michael, and a good-looking bastard as well; and Brian Running, a real man's man who always seemed to echo my thoughts exactly at the Amnesty Campaign meetings - where's the beer and is it a free bar?! All these characters are in the background of the film, but Ronnie knew then, as he does today, who is on his side; who has shown support throughout the long, tedious battle. Ronnie's memory is still razor sharp and he will never forget them - just wait until his eventual release.

The film features classic music tracks, and Max later told me that the songs were Ronnie's favourites. I had heard Ronnie talk about one of his favourites back in the 1990s - a beautiful song called 'The Flower Duet' by Delibes from the Opera *Lakmé*, composed in 1883. The song is incredibly powerful and relates so well to the Carlish images of Ronnie at the time of his 70th birthday. Another of the tracks, playing in the film when Ronnie, Bruce Reynolds and Dave Courtney are walking along the Brazilian beachfront, is 'Can't Take My Eyes Off of You' by Andy Williams. The next song on the soundtrack, although only released in 1978, was also one of Ronnie's all-time favourites - Sid Vicious (Sex Pistols) singing 'My Way'. Ronnie has always loved the punk sound and he loved the way this record starts slow and traditional and then suddenly bursts into life with the sound getting louder and more robust. He loved the Frank Sinatra original too, but was totally besotted with Sid's version. Max's film was promoted in the UK and Germany but was not a prolific seller, and has over the years become a very rare and collectable Ronnie Biggs item.

I found out later on that everyone at that party was absolutely petrified of Roy (Prettyboy) Shaw. Born in East London in 1936, Roy was initially a professional middleweight boxer, winning ten fights out of ten with six knockouts, but the pickings were better in the armed robbery game. In 1963 Roy was sentenced to 18 years' imprisonment for what was a record-breaking haul in an armed robbery on a security van, The judges must have thought that was the end of him - but they were so wrong. Roy exploded in prison. Attacks on prison officers and fights with other inmates with reputations were everyday occurrences and the system simply could not handle him. He saw the screws as the enemy and he was at war with them. They would tussle with Roy with their batons and shields over and over again, but it just made him more angry and more determined to win his war with them. Roy was totally out of control and uncontrollable. He was simply too violent for the system and therefore they shipped him off to Broadmoor Hospital for the criminally insane, where the 'liquid cosh' was waiting for him. Although now looking through a constant drug haze and sometimes barely able to stand due to the strength of the medication, he continued his war with the authorities and threw punches at the prison officers. Roy was kept in the dungeons or 'the hellhole' as they were referred to in Broadmoor Hospital. His days were spent locked away in solitary in total darkness, drugged up to the eyeballs and receiving electric shock treatment.

The turning point for Roy Shaw came when his old pal Joey Pyle visited him and told him straight the trouble that he was in, and that he would die in Broadmoor if he carried on his one-man war with the prison authorities. Fortunately, as people tend to do when Joe Pyle speaks to them, Roy listened to what he said and took it on board. From then on, he was on a different mission - to win his freedom. He settled down as best he could and was eventually released. Roy then faced a totally different problem: how was he going to earn money on the outside?

Roy (Prettyboy) Shaw became Britain's first unlicensed fighter and remains to this day the sport's most famous name. All Roy's fights were as legendary as his name soon became, beating other big names such as Lenny McLean, Ron (the Butcher) Stander, Donny (the Bull) Adams, etc. All the money Roy earned in these fights he wisely invested in property, and as a result he is doing very well even today (2008). Roy Shaw is the number one attraction at the boxing shows these days, but remains grounded and unfazed by the 'gangster-celebrity' craze. It's amazing when you consider that Roy was once Britain's most dangerous prisoner with little hope of release, and yet he turned his life around and is now a millionaire businessman driving a Bentley. I am sure you will agree that Roy Shaw is a man to be admired. No less than 35 respected faces have submitted tributes about Roy to his website to date, names that include Reggie and Ronnie Kray, Charlie Richardson, Joey Pyle Snr, Joey Pyle Jnr, Freddie Foreman, Howard Marks, Mad Frankie Fraser, Eric Mason, Charles Bronson, Stilks, Carlton Leach, Gypsy Johnny Frankham, Jimmy Stockin, Dave Courtney, Bruce Reynolds and, of course, Sir Ronnie Biggs - says it all, doesn't it?

Throughout 2001 and into 2002, I was supporting Michael Biggs where and whenever I could, and on Thursday 28 March 2002 Michael went to the Royal Courts of Justice, The Strand, London, together with his legal team, to lodge an application for a judicial review of the recent decision of the Criminal Cases Review Commission (CCRC) to refuse the application for Ronnie's case to go to the Court of Appeal.

It would be an understatement to say that it was an honour in early 2002 to meet Tel Currie and Roy Shaw in Belmarsh Visitors' Centre. I had noticed earlier a bright red Bentley Convertible approaching the visitors' car park, but hadn't realised that the Bentley, surrounded by all the Ford Mondeos, Vauxhalls and Nissans, actually belonged to Roy Shaw and was being driven by Tel Currie.

As we were all going through the usual security checks, I will always remember Roy telling me over and over that there was no way they were going to allow him through to see Ronnie. Believe me, he was getting very nervous about that fact, and I reassured him that everything would be fine. After all, I had informed Belmarsh's visiting office only a week earlier who would be visiting and had confirmed the date and time, and Roy had a visiting order to prove it. However, I can hardly imagine the strange position in which Roy felt at that time. His experiences had previously been as a guest of Her Majesty at one of her institutions rather than as a visitor. What I loved and admired about Roy on this visit, though, was his air of innocence and his total respect for what the prison officers requested of him during the security checks. He was, and is, a true gentleman, and he is someone that I am so proud to say is a real and greatly respected friend.

Roy hadn't seen Ronnie since his 70th birthday party back in 1999, and it was an emotional meeting, particularly under those circumstances. Although it ended with 'tears at bedtime' it was a great laugh, especially when Tel and I watched Ronnie (crippled with his walking stick) try to land a right-hander on the infamous Roy Prettyboy Shaw's mush. It was a hilarious thing to witness and Roy's response was, "Only Biggsy could ever get away with that."

The ultimate Belmarsh Boy was a Mr Harry Marsden, whom I had heard of - his legend went before him - but I had never met him. In 2004 Tel Currie telephoned me to ask if I could organise a visit for him, me and Harry Marsden. As with any of Tel's visiting order requests, I ran it by

Ronnie straight away. Tel knew these people really well even if I didn't, so I knew if he ever asked for permission for someone to visit Ronnie I knew they would be 100% genuine and I was very pleased to be able to get to know them. I always used to say, "Tel, if you and A.N. Other want to visit, I don't mind ducking out." However, his response was always, "Mike, you can read Ronnie's A-Z sheet even if it's upside down. That's why you need to be part of the visit." I really didn't mind, of course, although I have to say that on a lot of the Gray-Currie-Shaw visits - and there were plenty of those each year - sometimes I would ask Ronnie to spell out the sentence again only for Roy to get it the first time around. Ronnie's response would be a handshake for Roy and a look that said, "Roy, who are these two fucking young idiots?" (Yes, Tel, Ronnie meant us two!)

Ronnie had a great Belmarsh pal called Gary, who helped him with all his writing and reading and telephone calls, as well as chasing people up for visit confirmations, so I was relying on him to get the ball rolling on this visit. I only once had the privilege - and that's what it was - to shake Gary's hand as he left the visiting hall in 2002, and as I stood to shake his hand the prison officers shouted, "Sit down! Let go!" etc. We owe you, Gary, so a huge thank you from me, Tel, Roy and Harry - total respect. People don't realise that without you our visits would've taken so much longer to organise. I have always said that, should I ever write about Ronnie Biggs, then you would feature as a very big part of his HMP Belmarsh years. So God bless you, Gary, you're an absolute diamond - see you at Ronnie's parole party.

Anyway, back to Harry Marsden. I soon learnt from a letter I received from Ronnie that Ronnie and Harry had been in 'the Hate Factory' together, otherwise known as HMP Wandsworth. Ronnie had a lot of respect for 'H', as he called Harry in his letter to me. Harry Marsden was known to be the leader of the Geordie Mafia and ended up serving time for armed robberies, etc. I awaited Gary's call 24 hours later and gave him Harry Marsden's details, and a visit for the three of us was arranged for about five weeks' time.

At this time, Tel was gaining a reputation as a very accomplished journalist, as well as being a pal of almost every London underworld character you could think of and organizing boxing events. He had already had one book published called *Bouncers* (Milo Books, 2003), which he wrote with Julian Davies, and his second, brilliant book *Heroes and Villains: The Good, The Mad, The Bad and The Ugly* (Blake Publishing, 2005), written with Charlie Bronson, was in production. Ronnie actually contributed to Tel's second book, saying: "Both Tel Currie and Charlie Bronson have given me great support since my return to England in May 2001. As you may or may not know, I have not been in the best of health but am still kept as a Category A prisoner in HMP Belmarsh, South-east London. I correspond with them both as best I can on a regular basis even though I find it very difficult to write anything. I have read much of the book already and it is shaping up to be the only book of truth on all the Chaps of the Underworld. Love you Tel, Ronnie Biggs."

Great Train Robbery mastermind Bruce Richard Reynolds also said: "Charlie Bronson is a phenomenon in the prison system today, and Tel Currie's book will be a real eye opener to many people. Good luck, Tel. Respect as always, Bruce Reynolds."

Roy (Prettyboy) Shaw said of Tel Currie: "Both Charlie and Telboy [the nickname Roy calls him] are both close genuine friends of mine. I am not the sort of person who constantly has an entourage around him and I only choose to have a handful of close friends. I see Telboy more than I do Charlie. Tel is a strong and honest man with Old School principles, which commands much respect. He also respects others in return. I have been lucky enough to have read much of this book. Both Telboy and Charlie know what they are on about. It is indeed about The Chaps. Finally the truth. Enjoy. Roy Prettyboy Shaw."

Tel also paid me a very nice compliment by including me in the book, together with a photograph of me and Michael Biggs at Greg Foreman's boozer for Ronnie's wedding reception. To find my name among the underworld elite was indeed an honour and something I am very proud of today. Tel wrote:

"Mike Gray - Mike is indispensable and irreplaceable to Sir Ronnie Biggs. Mike is a close personal friend of the legendary Great Train Robber and is the figurehead of the campaign to release him (The Free Ronnie Biggs Campaign). When Ronnie decided to return to England in May 2001, Mike was alerted before the UK press/media, and Mike was also present at Ronnie's wedding in HMP Belmarsh in July 2002, an honour indeed as only ten guests were allowed to attend.

"People like Mike work tirelessly for their friends without fanfare and with little credit. In this world of sycophants, hangers-on, fame whores and reflected glory seekers, their type is very rare and very special and that's why people like Mike deserve a mention in this book, not just the main faces. Mike and Michael Biggs (Ronnie's son) have worked together on a Free Ronnie Biggs record and Mike is one of Ronnie's very few regular visitors. Let's hope the work, determination and loyalty of people like Mike Gray pay off and the government finds the heart to release Sir Ronnie Biggs."

Anyway, I digress, so back to the Gray-Currie-Marsden visit to Belmarsh to see Ronnie. I awaited the arrival of Tel and Harry in Belmarsh Visitors' Centre, where we had to check in. I was very surprised to see how healthy Harry looked after what Tel had told me about Harry fighting a losing battle with cancer, and Harry hadn't sounded very ill on the telephone when I called him only weeks earlier. But here he was - the man who told me that it was his dying wish to see face-to-face his old pal from Wandsworth Prison, Ronald Arthur Biggs. On meeting, Ronnie and Harry exchanged the complimentary, "You look fucking well, you old bastard!" Tel and I sat in awe of these two true crime legends as they talked about the old days in Wandsworth Prison in the '60s and the nicknames of some of the characters they knew and those they no longer wished to know. This was my first meeting with Harry Marsden and sadly it was to be my last. After the visit to Belmarsh, he wrote to thank me for organising it and that was the end of my contact with him. It was a sad day when Tel informed me that Harry had passed away in December 2007.

Another very sad passing in 2007 was Joey Pyle Senior, who died of natural causes. Joey was a total legend and an absolute diamond. He was always there to help and support us when we (the Free Ronnie Biggs campaign) needed him to help Ronnie and Michael Biggs with regard to setting up charity nights to raise money for the appeals, etc. Joe's funeral was held at Rose Hill, Surrey, only a mile or so from his home in Lower Morden Lane. Living close to Joe, I used to see him on a regular basis. Over 1,000 people attended the funeral service in February 2007 at St Theresa's Church. I had arranged to meet Michael Biggs at Morden Underground Station that day, as we were both representing the Biggs family, and while I was waiting for him to arrive, all kitted out in my black suit and Crombie, I soon found myself surrounded by a lot of people in the same attire. I met Howard Marks and pals among the many mourners, and everyone gathered at Joe's house before walking the short distance to the church behind the funeral procession.

Thursday 1st March 2007
A FINAL FAREWELL TO JOEY PYLE SENIOR
Dave Courtney along with 3,000 others flocked to Morden in Surrey to say goodbye to the legend Joey Pyle Snr yesterday.
Braving high winds, heavy rain and hailstones, over 300 walking mourners got off of 3 52-seater coaches and a fleet of minibuses to make the 1 mile journey on foot behind the procession that was made up off several members of the Outlaw Motorcycle Club on pristine bikes at the head, followed by 4 beautiful black horses dressed in full regalia drawing a large and ornate glass-sided Victorian carriage which contained the coffin. Next came 2 flower carrying funeral cars decorated

in a large Caesar's medallion and the words "MY PAL JOEY" spelt out in
flowers as well as many others. Behind those were 19 black official
funeral cars, 2 privately rented limos and 157 private cars.

Friends and family sent so many floral tributes they had to be delivered
to the church on a 32-foot artic trailer.

The church was packed to overflowing, so much so that the doors
couldn't be closed and hordes stood on the steps, squeezed together with
their heads cocked towards the open door to listen.

By the time of the second service at the cemetery, over 3,000 people
filled the graveyard and 76 cars were parked bumper to bumper all the
way up the drive and over 100 other cars filled the surrounding streets.
After a short service, all mourners braved the rain and strong winds to
trudge across the wet grass to the graveside to say their final goodbyes
to the legend that will always be Joey Pyle.

Dave would like to personally thank all of his boys who were our security
on the day and the 300 people who came from Camelot for the sad 5-
hour event. (Courtesy of Dave Courtney's website)

Michael and I chatted to Bruce and Nick Reynolds outside the church, and once inside I sat next to Gary Mason (one of our greatest heavyweight boxers) at the back of the packed building. After the service I spoke to Kenny Lynch on the way out of the church, Jimmy White mixed with mourners, and Michael and I also chatted to Jamie Foreman and ex-*Coronation Street* star Chris Quentin. It was a fantastic, respectful send-off for Joe, who never said no to our requests for help with the campaign. We're so grateful for everything he did for Ronnie and Michael Biggs.

Any future charity gatherings, underworld get-togethers, boxing functions, etc., will never be the same again without Joe there. Ronnie was very upset when he heard about Joe's passing. In Liam Galvin's gangster video, *Biggs Night Out 2*, Joe and the Chaps are all interviewed about Ronnie. I was interviewed outside The Park Tavern in Norwood, along with pub guv'nor Charlie Breaker, about Ronnie's treatment in Belmarsh, and it also features Tony Lambrianou, Cass Pennant, Tel Currie, Roy Shaw, Dave Courtney, Bruce Reynolds and pals. It's a great video/DVD. Even today (2008), I am still in regular e-mail contact with Charlie Breaker, someone I was introduced to in 2001 by Tel Currie and Nick Reynolds. Charlie always supported our Biggsy charity nights at his pub and is a very respected man in the underworld. Charlie has been there, seen it and done it loads of times. So respect him. Thanks again, Charlie, for all your support.

Throughout 2003 until 2007 when Ronnie was transferred to HMP Norwich, Tel Currie, Roy Shaw and I were Ronnie's most regular visitors, aside from Michael and family, which earned us the Biggsy nickname of The Three Stooges. The last visit we made together was in late 2006 and Ronnie told us that it was rumoured that he would be leaving Belmarsh in early 2007. Ronnie had been told similar stories before over the years, raising his hopes and then dashing them again, but this time Ronnie was very excited by the news given to him by his lawyer Giovanni di Stefano, and I had a feeling from him that maybe a move in 2007 could at last come to fruition as a result of Giovanni's hard work and efforts towards getting Ronnie transferred.

My last visit to see Ronnie in Belmarsh was with German Frank Werner in the spring of 2007. By this time Ronnie had been told officially by Miss Smith (new Home Secretary) that he would be transferred in the very near future, but to where no one knew, not even Ronnie. However, wherever it was, the Belmarsh Boys would follow.

Chapter 5
The Belmarsh Boys Go Visiting

(by Tel Currie)

When The Boys - Roy Prettyboy Shaw, Mike Gray and I - visited Ronnie Biggs at Belmarsh on 10 February 2006, Roy echoed what everyone was thinking when he said:

"Tel, look at the fucking state of Biggsy! What the fuck is he doing in here?"

Our visit had been scheduled for 2 p.m., but for some unexplained reason neither Ronnie nor any of the other prisoners were brought into the visiting room until 2.30 p.m., so everyone lost a full half-hour of visiting time. It may not sound a big deal, but when you only get a few visits from friends and family per month, 30 minutes makes a hell of a

difference and, of course, the time is not made up - the visit is still terminated at 4 p.m. prompt. After going through the extremely thorough searches, necessitating shoes, jackets, jewellery and jumpers to be removed, a good look in the mouth and under the tongue with a torch and the taking of fingerprints via an infrared finger-board, we all lined up on squares on the floor so that the highly trained dogs could sniff our bits as we waited to enter the visiting room.

In the visiting room we lined up again at a desk manned by prison officers, where we had to show our IDs and visiting orders and put our index fingers in yet another infrared fingerprint monitor. Then we were told the number of the area where we had to sit and wait for Biggsy - D1 in this case. On all our previous visits, Ronnie had already been seated in the assigned area waiting for us to join him, but today, as I said, we ended up having to wait half an hour for him to arrive. As the door opened and we saw our friend Biggsy for the first time in a couple of months I heard Roy gasp then mumble to himself under his breath and in shock, "Christ, look at 'im." Roy actually admitted that if he had been visiting on his own he would not have known which one Ronnie was!

I knew what he meant. This apparition before us looked nothing like the man we had seen on the last visit and was certainly not a bit like he looks in his famous photos. I was also totally in shock. Ronnie struggled with all his strength to raise his hand and give the three of us a feeble wave. Ronnie is a tall man but today he looked tiny, completely hunched up in his a prison-issue fluorescent orange bib. He wasn't wearing his false teeth, so his face looked older and more sunken than usual. It took him a while to reach us as he shuffled along in his slippers, wobbling slightly before regaining his balance. He was dribbling from the side of his mouth as a result of multiple strokes. Here, then, was an ill man in his mid-70s inside Europe's most secure prison and he was considered an escape risk!

Ronnie and I hugged first - a tight, emotional embrace, and I kissed him on the cheek and whispered a personal message in his ear. At least this was more intimate than my visits to Charlie Bronson, where you could only shake his hand through the bars. Then Ronnie and Roy embraced, and the fact that we had all seen Ron on previous visits didn't diminish the emotional power of these two men who genuinely loved each other. There was such a long history between them – first meeting while sewing mail bags 43 years earlier and now coming face to face again in such harsh surroundings and under such heartbreaking circumstances. Much tragedy had struck during that time, not least Ronnie's son Nicky being killed in a car accident in Australia.

Many people, who never bother to gain sufficient knowledge on a subject before proclaiming themselves experts (and there are millions of these people in every walk of life waffling on about every subject under the sun - you know the type), think that Ronnie Biggs's life on the run has been nothing but laughs, constant parties, unlimited money and an all-round care-free existence, but nothing could be further from the truth. Roy actually appeared on Kilroy (what a smug twat that Kilroy is!) in a programme about Ronnie. Now Roy has been to Ron's place in Rio and stayed there as a guest for a while, so he knows exactly what Ronnie's place is like. But on this show there were these complete twats telling Roy about the multimillion-pound mansion Ron lived in. When Roy told them he'd been there and that his home was far from a mansion, these idiots who had never been there told Roy he was wrong! I really do detest those types; they do my head in. Ronnie Biggs has had his share of pain, trust me.

So when these two old friends hugged, eyes did become moist. Ron steadied himself, sat down and took out a pen and paper for us and a letter sheet for himself. Since one of his strokes had robbed Ron of his speech, pointing at letters so that his visitors could write them down to form the words and sentences had become Ron's method of communication. After Ron had spelled out that he fancied going a few rounds with Roy (as he always does), we asked him if he had watched a TV programme the night before called *Kidnap Ronnie Biggs*, which charted a kidnap attempt in 1981 by a group of scum that included low-life John Miller, some big fat slag called Fred Prime, Tony Marriage and Patrick King. There may have been more, but they were such a bunch of filthy losers that I and I'm sure loads of others can't even remember their names. Obviously, being complete losers, they failed miserably, but not before causing a great deal of unnecessary distress and sadness for Michael Biggs, who was just a little five-year-old boy at the time and didn't know if he would ever see his beloved dad alive again. What brave men these were!

Ronnie had watched the programme and it had brought all the terrible memories flooding back. We could still see the anger in his eyes. Ronnie very rightly still despises those who kidnapped him, not for what they did to him but for how it scared his little boy. Anyone who knows Ron will tell you that hatred does not come easily to him. He is not and never has been a man full of anger or violence, but these cowards really flip his switch on, but it's hardly surprising. I don't know how much those bastards got paid for appearing on that programme, but it's disgraceful that they got a penny!

Then Roy told Ronnie a true story that really cheered Ron up. A few years back, Roy was at the Circus Tavern in Purfleet, Essex, watching a performance by Freddie Starr. He was sat enjoying the show when he recognised someone in the audience. Then it clicked - it was John Miller, one of the kidnappers! Roy darted over to him, hurling abuse on the way, and attacked Miller. He cracked him in the mouth, nutted him, picked him up and threw the slag out of the door! On hearing this, Ronnie's face burst into a huge toothless grin and he gave Roy a big thumbs-up. Then Ron grabbed his hand and shook it profusely with sheer delight. It gave Mike Gray and I great pleasure to hear that one as well, and especially to see Ron's beaming face even if it was only for a fleeting moment. Unbelievably and admirably, Ronnie Biggs still manages to see some joy in living.

One thing I find incredible is the number of people who stick Ronnie's name in their books and stories, telling everyone what great mates they were with Biggsy, and yet have never even tried to visit him when he needs them the most. Bruce and Nick Reynolds, Roy, Mike Gray and I, together with his son Mike of course, visit regularly, but not many others. There have also been a few people who have tried to visit Ronnie but whom Ron has refused to see because they are mongrels. I know a couple of them and they are well known for using the names of others to give themselves some credibility and to make some money from it. Ron's not stupid and always knocks these maggots back. By the way, before you accuse me of doing exactly that myself, I can assure you that Ronnie has personally given the go-ahead for any pieces about him in this book and he has also read them all. If he hadn't approved of something, then those sections would be omitted - simple as that. I can also tell you that everything I am writing here is 100% true.

There are still those, however, who go ahead anyway and mould the stories to suit themselves. The media also make things up about Ron and quote things that he never actually said. One of the most famous of these was when Ron was quoted as supposedly saying, "All I want is a nice pint of bitter in a pub in Margate." That has been pinned on Ron as one of his famous quotes, but it's bullshit! Ronnie Biggs never, ever said that. In terms of content and sentiment, of course, it's a harmless quote. What is disturbing, however, is the fact that the press can make something up, publish it and have the world believe that a certain person really did say it. It makes you wonder how many people the press have got sent down or even had hung because of their coverage of a case - scary thought.

Communicating with Ron through his letter sheet becomes easy after a while. I suppose it's a bit getting used to mobile phone texting. Using this letter pointing/sentence forming method, we discussed everything you could think of: Ronnie's old friends like Eric Flowers and Paul Seabourne; the difference between the older chaps and the newer ones; women; Brazil; terrorists; and, of course, the big question - what the hell was he doing in Belmarsh high-security prison? That was something none of us could answer - can you?

Ronnie showed us once again the painful-looking tube that goes directly into his stomach, his only means of nourishment. I was thinking how hellish it must be to hear and see everything going on around you (although his eyesight isn't good and his spectacles are stolen regularly) but not be able to it react to it. It must be like being in a coma but with your eyes open. He was also constantly dribbling and wiping his mouth, He doesn't have as much control over his body as he would like, and in prison especially you really want everything working fine just as a matter of survival.

So, our hour-and-a-half visit (which should have been two hours) was up, but before we left we said hello and goodbye to Gary, the prison friend that helps Ronnie read and write his letters, makes phone calls to Ronnie's friends and family with important messages, sorts out the visiting orders and generally keeps an eye out for Ron. Why does he do this? Simply because he's a good man. In this day and age, it's natural to be very suspicious of people who put themselves out for you and wonder what they're after, but there are still some good ones left who do things purely out of love and respect. Gary is one of those genuine ones.

We know that Ronnie Biggs will never give up - he's not the type. Despite his condition, his mind stays focused on the hope of a Home Secretary with a shred of human kindness deciding that his situation is silly and enough is enough, so that he can spend his final days in freedom. But there's no self-pity with this man, not an ounce. Ronnie's bodily mechanics may have betrayed him, but his spirit still exudes a joy for life. His heart is warm and his soul is filled with hope. He knows that if he gives up hope he'll die - it's as true and as simple as that.

As the officers screamed out for everyone to leave, we made another emotional farewell. Ron spelled out on his board: "Will you three please come again? Obviously we replied that we would keep on coming, and coming, until he was out of that godforsaken place. I'm not ashamed to say that I gripped Ron tightly and whispered in his ear that I loved him and that he would be out soon, and Roy and Mike did the same. It was hard to leave him because, to be blunt, with the poor state of his health you simply didn't know if that was the very last time you would ever see him. Ron waved to us from the moment we got up off the chairs, while we walked to the desk, while we queued to show our ID to get out again, right up until we were out of sight.

On our final visit to Belmarsh, we were even more disgusted at Ron's treatment than ever. Inmates were only allowed two hours for a visit, so every second was priceless. On this occasion Ronnie was wheeled into the visiting room in a wheelchair, looking even more frail than before. He gave us a wave, but was then wheeled straight past us and through a side door where the 'normal' prisoner's were coming out. Ron emerged again twenty minutes later wearing an orange bib - obviously he was an escape risk!

So that was twenty minutes hacked off the visit. Roy and I lifted Ron from his wheelchair onto one of the chairs and, despite his physical deterioration, Ronnie's amazing spirit shone through and he was on good form. As usual, he squared up to Roy and proceeded to have a mock knuckle fight. He took the piss out of all and sundry, including us and the screws.

If the authorities think they can break his spirit, they are wasting their time. He may be fading physically, but within that shell is a man of steel, a natural born rebel. Ronnie is basically a loveable rogue. He's not a man of violence and never has been - and he's certainly not going to start now! Of course, many of the men I know are men of violence - it's part of their profession - but men like Bruce Reynolds and Ronnie Biggs are certainly not of that ilk. Bruce was a man of cunning and brainpower and Biggsy was just a cheeky rascal. When Biggsy went over the wall at Wandsworth he made it clear that no weapons were to be used during the escape and nobody was to be hurt. When Ronnie found out that one of the lads had gone against his wishes and was indeed was carrying a weapon, Ron went mental.

People who knew Ronnie in Brazil have told me that he always said. " I will find out who my real friends are when I return to England. As it stands, apart from his son Mike, Roy, Mike Gray and I are Ron's most regular visitors. And, just for the record, I want to make it clear that I asked both Ronnie and Mike Biggs if it would be okay to write this, and they both said yes. Otherwise I wouldn't have written it. I never want to be tarred with the same brush as a lot of these prats who have jumped on the Kray name. I would never be so disrespectful. Ronnie's brain is still as sharp as a tack and he wants me to write the TRUTH about him.

As I said, Ronnie now points to letters on a chart to make words and that's how we communicate. The good thing about that is there's no small talk, no bullshit or wasted words; everything is relevant. So there's no talking about the weather! You would be amazed how many topics can be covered with this restricted method of communication.

At the end of the visit, we lifted Ron back into his wheelchair, his bib was removed and the screws wheeled him out and back to his cell.

The three of us were totally silent as we made our way out of the prison. The looks on our ashen faces said what we were all thinking: could that have been the last time we would see Ronnie alive?

If they release this sick old man now, the government may gain some much-needed respect. If they don't, then mark my words: when Ron passes away they will have created a martyr, and forever more the history books will describe them as revenge-obsessed tyrants.

Chapter 6
Wedding Bells
(by Mike Gray)

On 10 July 2002, Ronald Arthur Biggs married for the second time in his life. His bride on this occasion was Raimunda Rothen (Michael's mother) and the wedding took place in the very unusual surroundings of the UK's most secure prison, HMP Belmarsh.

Ronnie had long divorced his former wife Charmian, now called Charmian Brent, who continued to stay and live her normal life in Melbourne, Australia, as she had done since Ronnie went on the run in 1970, heading for South America and later Brazil. Charmian visited Ronnie on numerous occasions after his re-arrest in Rio de Janeiro by Scotland Yard detectives in February 1974. She again flew out to see him in the mid-'80s and Ronnie declared his love for her again and wanted her to stay in Brazil and start a new life out there with him. However, Charmian's two sons, Christopher and Farley, were not keen on the idea, as they both felt that Ronnie had treated their mother very poorly. As a result, Charmian remained in Australia and has enjoyed a very comfortable lifestyle with her sons, and has recently become a grandmother again.

Since Ronnie's return to the UK in 2001, I had been in regular e-mail and telephone contact with Charmian, but when Ronnie married Raimunda everything went quiet. However, on one of my visits to see Ronnie I persuaded him to send Charmian a note to say he was thinking of her, etc., to try to break the ice. I sent her an e-mail to let her know that Ronnie would be making contact via the Royal Mail (who else?) I could tell from Charmian's reply that she knew about Ronnie's inability to write or even post a letter, but that she was secretly optimistic that it might happen and end the silence between them, which I know for a fact lasted three years.

In September 2001, Ronnie was yet again rushed from HMP Belmarsh to Woolwich's Queen Elizabeth Hospital, this time with internal bleeding. As a result, Michael Biggs and I spent that evening exchanging mobile phone calls and text messages to keep abreast of the situation and offer moral support. It was not long, however, before the radio breakfast shows were letting millions of listeners throughout the world know that Ronnie Biggs was almost dead - their words not mine. On hearing and reading the speculation and rumours, I telephoned Charmian in Australia. It was 8 a.m. in the UK, so it must have been 6 p.m. in her part of the world. Sure enough, she had heard on the Aussie radio stations that Ronnie was in hospital again, but what she didn't realise was that this time it was serious.

I told Charmian what the doctors had told Michael, and she was so grateful for my being considerate and thinking of her, but that's the relationship I have always had with her and will continue to do so. Also I was doing it for Ronnie and the Biggs family. She was actually playing bridge with two close friends when I called, and she told me she awaiting an operation on her hip, which was very painful and uncomfortable. I would e-mail her with any other news, and vice versa, and I would always print out her communications and post them on to Ronnie in prison. That is something I have done since 2001 and still do today (2008). I do the same with Ronnie's old pal in Rio de Janeiro, Johnny Pickston. I mail him when I get a visiting order and ask him if he has any 'Rio gossip' for Ron, so I can print out his news and send it on to Ronnie.

Johnny Pickston was Ronnie's best mate in Rio, and he and his wife Lia looked after little Michael Biggs when Ronnie was kidnapped by certain scumbags in 1981. Lia went on to write a book in Brazil about her experiences of looking after the world's most famous criminal's son, not knowing at the time if Ronnie would be sent back to the UK. In the event, Ronnie was landed on Barbados and the courts returned him to Brazil to be with his son Michael.

So as the weeks passed, Charmian sent e-mail updates from her side of the world and I reciprocated with news of the Free Ronnie Biggs campaign, stories in the UK press and, of course, the fallout from the prison wedding. When I say 'fallout', I don't mean the ongoing arguments/sulks between Charmian and Ron, I mean the Michael Biggs passport story and the 'Ronnie's wife elopes to Switzerland' and the wedding photos rumours, etc.

On Thursday 9 July, the UK's national newspapers were drooling at the prospect of a juicy exclusive on the 'Train Robber's Prison Wedding'. A family spokeswoman (Judy Totton, who was actually Ronnie and Michael's PR) announced the planned wedding ceremony, which would be a small affair to be attended by Ronnie's son Michael, his girlfriend Veronica and their two-year-old daughter Ingrid, plus a handful of very close family friends. The papers said that Ronnie had proposed not less than four times to Raimunda, and on this point they had their facts correct. On a visit Ronnie once told me that it was four times and said he might even make it five, but if she didn't say yes after that he was going to give up trying. He used to tell me that he was still a good catch, so I used to say to him, "Biggsy, you have been well and truly caught".

Raimunda Rothen had caught Ronnie Biggs's eye 31 years earlier in a cabaret club in Rio, and for three years he hid his true identity from her, instead adopting the name 'Mike Haynes', who was in fact a good friend of Ronnie's when he and Charmian lived in Australia between 1965 and 1970. It was the birth of their son Michael that saved Ronnie in 1974 from the clutches of Scotland Yard detectives, as local Brazilian law prevented the extradition of someone that was the father of a Brazilian child. Raimunda actually took a huge risk in having the baby, as doctors had advised that her continuing with the pregnancy could threaten both her health and that of her unborn child. However, she took the gamble so that Ronnie wouldn't be taken away.

At the time of the wedding, Raimunda was aged 54 and had lived in

Switzerland since the mid-1970s, but she had visited Ronnie in Belmarsh several times since his return in 2001. Judy Totton explained that Raimunda was extremely concerned about Ronnie's ailing health and accepted his proposal as she feared his life was drawing to a close. Ronnie was reportedly delighted that Raimunda had finally agreed to marry him, as he believed this was the best way of keeping the family together.

Michael Biggs had Brazilian citizenship and was awaiting news on his British passport application, which was being reviewed in light of the wedding and human rights legislation on the protection of family life. Michael's aim was to be able to travel freely between Brazil and the UK, and it now looked promising. A Home Office spokesperson confirmed that under the British Nationality Act (1981) his parents' marriage should entitle him to a passport. Of the marriage, Michael said: "We're all very happy and I'm very grateful to the prison service for allowing my father to fulfil one of his last wishes, so he may marry my mother Raimunda Rothen."

I spoke to Michael almost ten times a day leading up to the wedding. He kept saying he was so nervous that he felt like he was the one getting married. With only 24 hours to go until the ceremony, Michael called me to notify me that we would all be meeting at Belmarsh's Visitors' Centre, so that we could all check in with the prison authorities. He reminded me not to forget the usual ID documents, as the procedure would be just the same as on a normal visit, and we spoke about UK press speculation regarding 'The Big Ten'. Most of the national newspapers had reported that the Governor of Belmarsh had authorised only ten guests to attend the wedding at the prison chapel, and that figure included the bride herself. Taking into account family members, I was very honoured and proud to be informed by Michael that Ronnie had chosen all ten guests, each for a very specific reason, and that I was one of the ten.

At around 3 p.m. that Tuesday, the Big Ten list was made public knowledge by Judy Totton. The names were posted on her website: 1 -

Michael Biggs; 2 - Veronica (Michael's girlfriend); 3 - Ingrid (Michael's daughter); 4 - Mike Gray (me!); 5 - Judy Totton; 6 and 7 - One Armed Kev and his young lady Kerry from Bristol (close pals of Ronnie from the Rio days); 8 and 9 - Richard Mallett and Kirsty (Ronnie's legal team); and 10 - last but not least - the bride Raimunda Rothen.

Slowly but surely, the wedding details started appearing on other websites around the globe. The Media Circus was beginning to step up a gear, and throughout that Tuesday evening my phone was buzzing with calls from Radio London, BBC Plymouth (why Plymouth I don't know), GLR and many other talk-show stations, all looking for that different angle on the wedding story. I must admit that on the back of the wedding the Free Ronnie Biggs campaign got some much-needed widespread publicity. *The Guardian* gave us some excellent national coverage as well as other papers with a wide readership. That said, the morning couldn't come soon enough.

I arrived at Plumstead train station at 9 a.m. on the wedding day. Michael had told us all to be at Belmarsh Visitors' Centre by 10 a.m., and it was around a 20-minute walk to the prison from the station. A 20-minute walk in the opposite direction would have taken me to the front door of the Chestnut Rise home of Mr Dave Courtney, one of Plumstead's most famous personalities. As I turned the corner to walk past the entrance to Belmarsh Crown Court I could see a line of large lorries belonging to Sky TV, ITN and the BBC, and as I entered the driveway to the prison I was stopped by two prison officers, both for some strange reason decked out in blue polo shirts with matching blue boiler suit strides and Doc Martens. Hello, I thought, is this the SAS or what?

"Sorry, sir, could you please explain what you are doing in the prison grounds? Are you staff or a legal visitor? It's just that the Visiting Centre doesn't open for another two hours."

I was shocked by the questioning, but also angry at their assumption that I was either a brief or a casual prison worker. I was wearing my suit and tie, but after all it was a wedding I was supposed to be attending.

I produced from my pocket my official Belmarsh letter, bearing the signature of the Governor, which stated that I (Mike Gray), described on the invite as a close family friend, was authorised to be admitted into the prison grounds for the wedding of Prisoner 002731 (or, to you and me, Ronnie Biggs).

"Okay, sir," was the polite reply, and my name was ticked off the list on his clipboard. "If you would be so kind as to take the visitors' path to the Visiting Centre."

I really wanted to give him the flippant reply of: "You mean the same walk I take every two months when I visit and have taken for the past 14 months?" But no, nothing would spoil this special Biggsy Day, not even a sarcastic screw trying his utmost to provoke me. All I could think of was: why the blue outfits? Was it so that the wedding wouldn't seem so 'security surrounded' and would create a softness of image? Yes, that was it, I concluded. And my deductions were correct, as after post-ceremony photographs had been taken at the prison entrance I asked Mr Clipboard about it. But, fair play to him, he apologised for seeming rude and explained that they had been warned that members of the UK media were out in force and in disguise and would stop at nothing to clinch that big 'Wedding Exclusive'.

When I arrived at the Visitors' Centre I was greeted by a female officer, also dressed in her blues. All we needed was Shakin' Stevens to start belting out a song, and it would look like a set from *Grease*. I was asked to take a seat and it was explained that once all ten guests had congregated the usual security checks would be performed. It was treated just the same as a regular prison visit, except that this time we would be heading for the chapel instead of into the main prison complex.

Within 45 minutes of my arrival, and very nearly spot on 10 a.m., everyone was present and correct. Veronica and Ingrid gave me the Brazilian double kiss and a hug, as did Raimunda, whom I had seen only five days earlier at Michael's Old Street flat. I was introduced to Ronnie's legal team and also to Kevin and Kerry, none of whom I'd met before. I knew Judy from previous meetings and court appearances (not mine - Michael's deportation appeal). Michael was as casually dressed as he was every day. He had a 'no problem, all in good time, relax, take it easy' kind of attitude to life. He hadn't even bothered with a tie. I knew that Daddy (Ronnie) would have something to say about that!

We all went through the customary security procedures and then, just as everything seemed to be running as smooth as Ronnie's escape from Wandsworth all those years ago, a problem - a real big fucking problem - reared its ugly head.

A voice piped up loudly: "I MUST be on the list. Why am I not on the list? Michael, can you do something?"

In a matter of minutes all hell broke loose. One of the people in the Visiting Centre, whom I did not know or recognise, was a Mr Neil Silver from Virgin Books. He had only recently published a book with Michael and Ronnie, but he was not on the guest list for the wedding.

Then, after a 15-minute delay, one of the officers very clearly delivered one of those all-time classic one-liners: "If your name's not on the list, you ain't coming in."

And that was that. Mr Silver was left behind in the Visiting Centre, as the chosen ten were led to the prison's main gate and straight through security, which wasn't in operation, to the inner prison and up a flight of stairs to the chapel.

Greeting us at the door was Tony Jarman (Registrar for the London Borough of Greenwich) along with four prison officers, two in blues and the other two in the traditional prison officers' attire. We took our seats in the very small chapel and I noticed a table laid out with sandwiches, crisps and soft drinks (nice touch, Guv). Ronnie was led in by an officer and we all stood as he slowly made his way to his position next to Raimunda. Ronnie grunted when asked, "Do you take this woman?" and, as humorous as usual, his left hand squeezed Raimunda's arse, which brought hoots of laughter from those watching them, including the Registrar and the officers. Ronnie confirmed his reply by pointing to the 'yes' card held by the Registrar, and on the wedding certificate Ronnie placed a cross, as his handwriting was so poor due to his strokes.

Raimunda gave her occupation as a cleaner and Ronnie stated that he was a carpenter, as this was his trade in his hometown of Redhill, Surrey, in the years leading up to the Train Robbery of 1963. Ronnie gave his address as Belmarsh, Western Way, Thamesmead (the prison's official address).

The service took roughly 30 minutes to conclude, and then Ronnie and his new bride posed for photographs. Standing proud in his smart grey made-to-measure suit (WE know who bought it for him, but we won't say), Ronnie looked like an underworld godfather, but he still managed to keep us entertained. Raimunda, still looking a very sexy lady even at 54, didn't realise that as the camera snapped away Ronnie was busy dropping his false teeth! But that's why we all love him so much. His wicked sense of humour has never deserted him, and I doubt it ever will.

The officers took 30 photographs of the wedding ceremony and guests, but these remain the property of the Home Office to this day and will only be released when Ronnie gets his freedom. However, I am sure that they will be worth a fortune to a newspaper/media company looking for a very rare Exclusive that was only witnessed by a few.

After sandwiches and coffee we were all ushered out of the chapel, and ten minutes later we were all gathered outside the prison for Michael and Raimunda's media extravaganza to explode into action. It seemed as though the world's media were there, all with four-foot lenses on their Nokias.

Raimunda showed off her wedding ring for the press to admire and said, "I am very happy." Although they would never be able to consummate their marriage while Ronnie remains in prison, Raimunda was planning to visit him on a regular basis.

Michael said, "We are all together now. It was a short family ceremony. Very nice, with a lot of love. We're very happy the family is reunited once again." When asked about his deportation case, he added, "I'm just taking it one day at a time. Today I'm just happy for my parents."

By 11.45 a.m. everyone had dispersed from the scene, leaving the camera crews packing up their equipment. We all headed off into central London, and I travelled with Kevin and Kerry. When we arrived at The Punchbowl in Mayfair, a beautiful, small, traditional pub in the backstreets of Green Park owned by Gregg Foreman (London underworld legend Freddie Foreman's son, the TV and camera crews were already there and Michael was being interviewed live on the BBC's lunchtime news channel. Gregg did a great job of keeping the press out of the pub, although with all the London underworld characters that were arriving I think they thought better of it anyway.

The Punchbowl was built in the 1750s and is the second oldest pub in Mayfair, the oldest being The Guinea. Window boxes and hanging baskets adorn the outside, whilst inside is a simply furnished single bar, with bare floorboards and timber paneling and a spacious dining area at the rear, serving pub fayre at reasonable prices. The beers are very good too!

As we entered the pub, Bruce and Nick Reynolds were the first to hug the wedding party in celebration. Following close behind us were Tony Lambrianou, Joey Pyle, Brian Stone, Mr Davey and, of course, Freddie Foreman. The drinks were flowing all afternoon and no one paid for anything. After an hour of chatting and interviews and photos, Gregg shouted that dinner was served and everyone squeezed into the eating area. The catering team had done Ronnie and Raimunda proud. Michael gave a short toast and thanked each and everyone of us for turning up.

I found myself sitting next to a fella wearing a baseball cap, who was very quiet although he seemed to know all the faces there. It wasn't until he took off his cap that I realised just who it was - Brian Stone. I had met Brian nine months earlier at the Queen Elizabeth Hospital while visiting

Ronnie. Brian was the man responsible for fighting with the prison officer while Ronnie went up the rope ladder and away to freedom.

I have always said that Brian was an unsung hero, and he was telling me about a recent job he'd had as Charlie Kray's driver. But as quickly as Brian had arrived he was on his way again. He shook my hand and told me to say hello to Ronnie and let him know that Brian Stone was at his wedding reception. His presence there was a great honour indeed for Ronnie and a sign of a true friendship between them. After the meal, I ended up chatting to Tony Lambrianou and Mr Davey about the wedding ceremony and Ronnie's overall well-being while in Belmarsh Prison.

Tony was looking as immaculate as ever. He was always the perfect gentleman and he was well respected wherever he went. He was brought up with the Kray twins (Ronnie and Reggie) in Bethnal Green, East London, The East End of London was renowned for the criminals it turned out and several key firms developed among the youth: the Richardsons, the Nash brothers, the Krays and the Lambrianou brothers. They ran the system and that's how it had to be in those days, In 1969, Tony was convicted along with the Kray twins for the murder of Jack the Hat McVitie. He was a big man - six feet two inches tall and weighing sixteen stone, so he wasn't the sort of man you would want to upset in any way. He was given a 15-year recommendation and had no parole, serving 15 years and another 15 months as well, 12 of those years as a Category A prisoner.

I also spoke to Joey Pyle Snr, whom I had known for a long time as he lived only about a mile from my home, along with Mitch Pyle. Joey was saying how Ronnie should've stayed in Brazil as this country had nothing to offer him, and you couldn't help but agree with his sentiments. We discussed the local boozers in Morden and north Cheam, such as Tones and Jolsons, which were both regular haunts of his and were usually where he chose to be interviewed by the media. That way it gave the TV company what they wanted and also gave the bar a free bit of publicity. That was typical of Joe - very generous, and like Tony he was a real gentleman too.

I mentioned to Joe that my eldest son, who was still living at home with us, would be 21 very shortly and Joey said that he would pop round for a drink. Sure enough, as promised, when the day arrived Joey turned up on that Saturday night with Mitch to wish my son a happy 21st birthday. We all had a few drinks and then Joey went on to another engagement. And just to prove to you what a diamond he really is, the topic of conversation was about how he takes his two dogs over to the park, but the dogs are a Poodle and a Boxer - a very strange combination.

Joey Pyle organised our first Ronnie Biggs charity night in Reunion Jacques Bar in Twickenham and then quickly organised a second charity night at Charlie Breaker's pub, the Park Tavern in Norwood, South London. Both of these events were filmed by our good pal Liam Galvin, who runs Gangster videos, and can be found on his website. The atmosphere is superbly captured on film by Liam, accentuated by the superb backing tracks, and they really take you back. As always, the charity nights are like an underworld A-Z, courtesy of Joey's kind invitation, and they are fantastic nights for everyone to enjoy, whether members of the general public or underworld faces; everyone is welcome. I can never thank Joey enough for all the support he gave to the Biggsy campaign.

These events would raise funds for Michael to pay Ronnie's legal expenses as his case went through appeal after appeal. As we all know, lawyers don't come cheap! The charity night for Ronnie at Charlie Breaker's pub was very special, Dave Courtney became the auctioneer, selling off signed books, documents, photos, etc., and Bruce Reynolds (the Great Train Robbery mastermind and lifelong buddy of Ronnie) was actually signing anything and everything requested by people, even if they were personal items. A photograph or signature was never ever a problem to any of these guys.

Joey was a great and totally respected man, with a larger-than-life personality and a 'been there, seen it, done it' attitude (because he had).

Joe was great friends with the Krays and the Richardsons, and was also good pals with Roy Shaw, Lenny McLean and Freddie Foreman. In the so-called underworld Joe had no enemies. He always saw the advantages of peace over mindless violence for violence's sake. Roy Shaw will tell you that Joey Pyle literally saved his life three or four times over, and it was because of Joe's involvement that Roy finally saw the light. Joe also stood by Dave Courtney. He also worked tirelessly for sick and underprivileged children among many other good causes and frequently visited a children's hospice called Zoe's Place with some of the other Chaps. He even wrote a book called *Looking at Life* and gave every single penny he made from it to Zoe's hospice. At the same time, he exposed the huge companies that had made vast fortunes from children's products but refused to give anything back. As I said, he was a real diamond.

I chatted to Freddie Foreman at the wedding reception in his son's pub, and he was telling me how Gregg had always been into running his own pubs and before that one he'd had a pub in Kent. He said that Gregg wanted to turn the upstairs into a restaurant, and rather than explain it further he took me upstairs to the very old dining room, which resembled a Hammer House of Horror film set. The idea was to free up more space downstairs so that the bar area could be enlarged. It seemed weird that there I was, talking to someone I hardly knew, apart from his nicknames Brown Bread Fred and London Godfather, about dining rooms and food! Again, as with Joey Pyle, Freddie has that certain air about him and is a perfect gentleman, but you must always show him total respect. He's another lovely fella who is totally supportive of our Free Ronnie Biggs campaign and always gives his backing to anything Biggsy.

Freddie Foreman was born in South London in 1932 and served nine months in Wandsworth Prison for armed robbery in 1952. By 1956 Freddie had his own Firm, which included Buster Edwards and Tommy Wisbey (both subsequently in the Great Train Robbers gang) and others, and he was asked to take part in the Train Robbery but declined. In 1960, he was associated with Ronnie and Reggie Kray and their war with the Richardsons. When Ronnie Biggs escaped from Wandsworth on 8 July 1965, Freddie provided him with a safe house, and the following year he arranged a deal whereby Buster Edwards agreed to hand himself in to Scotland Yard in exchange for a lighter sentence, which he did on 19 September. Freddie was involved in organising a robbery of millions of pounds from Security Express in London, after which he fled the country and subsequently lived in Marbella in Spain for several years. Eventually the Spanish authorities caught up with him and he was extradited to the UK in July 1988. Although found not guilty of participating in the robbery, he was convicted of laundering the stolen cash and was sentenced to nine years in April 1990. He proved himself a model prisoner and helped to resolve a prison riot in Full Sutton. He was eventually released from Maidstone Prison in Kent in 1995 and was a pall-bearer at Ronnie Kray's funeral in March of that year. It is alleged that the main character played by Bob Hoskins in the film *The Long Good Friday* (1980) is based on Freddie's life story.

Another of Freddie's sons, Jamie Foreman (born in 1958), is today one of the UK's most popular actors and has appeared in various television and film epics, his most recent and better known roles being Duke in *Layer Cake* (2004) and Bill Sykes in Roman Polanski's *Oliver Twist* (2005). He also played opposite Ray Winstone and Kathy Burke in Gary Oldman's *Nil by Mouth*, as well as featuring in *Sleepy Hollow* and *Elizabeth*. In 2006 he appeared in the Doctor Who episode 'The Idiot's Lantern' and he also played a taxi driver in the cult film *The Football Factory*. Recent radio credits include the title role in *Wes Bell* by Matthew Broughton and the six-part series Hazelbeach by David and Caroline Stafford. He also played a minor role in *I'll Sleep When I'm Dead*.

Jamie is always very welcoming and you cannot help but like him straight away even if you don't know him. I was in his company both at Tony Lambrianou's funeral in 2005 and Joey Pyle's in February 2007, where

Michael Biggs and I represented the Biggs family. At the latter funeral, Michael and I were about to leave Joe's house in Lower Morden Lane to follow the hundreds of cars that had gathered, when Jamie came sprinting along the road and asked us which was Joe's house. I answered, "You've been here before with your dad, Jamie. Don't you remember?" In response said that whenever he and his dad visited Joe's house, he was so pissed by the time he left that he hadn't a clue where he was! It was a little bit of humour on a very sad day. God rest your soul, Joey.

I took my wife to the Joey Pyle Testimonial at Caesars Palace nightclub in Streatham, South London, on 19 February 2006. Little did anyone know at that time that within 12 months Joey would've passed away. The evening in honour of Joey had been arranged to celebrate his life and all that he had achieved, not only personally but also for other people. Attendees included "Celebrities from the Glamour world, the Film world, the Music world and, of course, guests from the Underworld". These were the exact words used on the £50 tickets, and I still have ours to remind us of a great evening's entertainment.

My wife Lita and I booked a table in the balcony at Caesars for the two of us plus my eldest son and his close friend Mark Ferguson (brother of *Big Brother*'s Bubble) and also Michael Biggs. This was the most special and memorable evening I have ever had. If only Ronnie could've been there, he would've been overwhelmed. We mixed freely and socialised between stage acts, which included The Odd Balls and American soul legend Jocelyn Brown, with none other than Dave Courtney compering and raising loads of money for Joey and his charities.

I introduced Lita to Roy Prettyboy Shaw, who was as polite as usual in acknowledging our presence. It was only the previous week that Roy, Tel Currie and I had visited Ronnie in HMP Belmarsh. Joey was not looking very well, but his firm handshake showed his inner strength in the same way as Ronnie's always did, despite his physical frailty. We then chatted to various celebrities, such as Bill Murray (*Eastenders*), Chris Quentin

(*Coronation Street*), Jimmy White (snooker legend), Alan Minter (one of our greatest boxers), Gary Bushell (TV critic and band member of The Gonads), Michael Greco (*Eastenders*) and Jamie Foreman (top actor), as well as well-known names from the underworld, such as Charlie Breaker, Charlie Richardson, Johnny Nash and many others. Dave Courtney estimated that there were around 1,200 people in the audience. It was a fantastic evening and one that I doubt we will ever see the likes of again.

I would like to thank Joey Pyle Jnr, whom I have got to know over the years and who has always supported our Ronnie Biggs charity nights and was ever present with his dad. One of Joey's last efforts on our behalf was when he was promoting a boxing night at Caesars and he e-mailed me to say that he was going to try to raise a few quid for the Ronnie Biggs campaign. I remember when I was chatting to him at our charity night in 2002 at Charles Breaker's boozer, he said that he could really relate to Michael's passion and love for his father, just like Joey Jnr with his own father. I will always remember his comments and feel proud that I can use them in my book. Take care, Joey, and thank you for all your kindness,

As the sun began to set on that warm July evening in 2002 after Ronnie's wedding reception, I started to say my farewells to Gregg and his team and Joey and Tony, plus others who were still in the bar with celebratory flowers in their lapels. It had been a very enjoyable and memorable day for all. On the tube journey home, I read the account of the day in the *Evening Standard* and found the incorrectness of the details laughable, but being the first newspaper to get the story out on the streets, they had the advantage over the dailies, which would not surface until the early hours of the following day.

The headline in the *Sun* newspaper the next day read: "I Do Ron Ron". It gave the wedding a three-page colour special editorial spread. Well, they had got the publicity on Ronnie's return home, but will they get the rights to the prison wedding photographs?

Chapter 7
A Criminal Record
with a Difference
(by Mike Gray)

It was mid-2004 and Ronnie was still banged up in HMP Belmarsh with nothing much happening on the legal front regarding his release or parole. I was still visiting Ronnie with Michael Biggs and Frank Werner, along with Roy Prettyboy Shaw and Tel Currie. It was now the norm for Michael to look after his own visiting orders for his family, etc., and I would take care of those for Ronnie's friends, past and present. As Ronnie had now been back inside for over three years, I just kept feeling that I could do more to help my old pal. On numerous occasions I wrote letters to Her Majesty the Queen as well as to the Home Secretaries David Blunkett and Charles Clarke, but both seemed to be a complete waste of time. However, I would not give up.

I was lucky, as I was on the outside enjoying my life whereas poor old Ronnie, now nearly 75 years of age, was still banged up in a cell for almost 23 hours a day, constantly getting his glasses, watch or CD batteries nicked by some bastard or other. He had no television in his cell in the Healthcare Centre. All 16 cells shared a TV room, but Ronnie found it virtually impossible to see the television from his wheelchair, never mind hear it. Ronnie therefore sought pleasure from his music and his collection of 12 CDs became his life. Belmarsh had a strict rules about what could be posted to the prison. Only letters and cards were acceptable, and other items (e.g. stationery, CDs, books, etc.) were a strict no-no. All monies had to be sent to the Governor in the form of a postal order or cheque, and when cleared or cashed the funds would be inserted into the prisoner's funds (i.e., regular pocket money).

Outrage is the only word we could use to describe Ronnie's current situation. Was the Home Office looking to keep him in Belmarsh high security for five years? No one knew the answer, but at least it was a benchmark to aim for. However, with no encouraging news forthcoming, in May 2004 Michael Biggs was invited onto BBC Radio to be interviewed on a programme called *Hardtalk*. Michael, as always, was obliging in agreeing to the interview so that he could raise questions in the media regarding his father. Michael put particularly strong emphasis on the fact that Ronnie was too old and too ill to be in prison and that in this day and age such draconian treatment should be reserved for the likes of scum such as double child killer Ian Huntley or Yorkshire Ripper Peter Sutcliffe. The interview was also shown on BBC TV around the world. As we all know, when interviewed live the aim of the questions thrown at you is often to try to make you look stupid. However, Michael remained calm, articulate, polite and truthful, so the media didn't get the reaction or answers that they were expecting or had hoped for. It was the same when I was interviewed live on SKY TV on Ronnie's return in 2001. The reporter conducting the interview looked at me and said, "You're wearing a suit." What did he expect - a Sex Pistols T-shirt with "Cosh the driver" on it and me talking as if I were Alf Garnett's son?!

It was almost June 2004 and I was travelling to work on the train when I had a thought about a criminal record - but in this case a vinyl one that we could sell. The idea was that it would make a much wider range and larger number of people aware of our struggle, which is exactly what it was at that time. Who knows, I thought, maybe we could even find a John Peel character who would stick his neck on the line and promote it? With these thoughts racing around in my head, I started to link words into sentences and then sentences into verses. I knew I had something that would raise awareness of Ronnie's plight, and if we could make some money on the back of it then the campaign would benefit financially as well. Happy days.

The first person I e-mailed was Frank Werner (German Frank), as he was well known to all the Biggs family. Frank had been a regular visitor to Ronnie's house in Rio de Janeiro, and although he lived in Munich he would always find both the time and finances to travel to see Ronnie. Thus over the years they had developed a great and close friendship. It was through Ronnie that I had first contacted Frank in 2001. Although Frank had a day job as a Finance Controller, he also had a punk band in Munich called Rauschangriff, which translates into English as 'Paralytic'. My idea was to write the lyrics myself and ask Frank to write the music, add the vocals and record the songs in the local studio that his band used on a regular basis for rehearsals. I had already decided that it would take the form of an EP with at least four tracks, so that the punters would feel as though they were getting value for money and would hopefully enjoy at least one of the tracks.

I could already see the record in the Top 50 Indie chart: an EP giving the campaign a worldwide voice and telling the story of Ronald Arthur Biggs, a grandfather in the UK's most secure prison and serving a 30-year sentence dished out to him over four decades earlier; a man just waiting to die. This project had to work, and I was determined to do everything possible to make sure it did.

Within 24 hours of this idea popping into my head, I had written down numerous verses for the songs, the first one entitled 'It's so harsh in Belmarsh'. It told the story of the very tough regime in Belmarsh prison, the conditions on visits and why the inmates are made to suffer. All the song lyrics tell their own story of Ronnie's hardships and life on the run - a life that reads rather like a potential film script for a James Bond movie. Just look at the facts: involved in the biggest cash robbery the country has ever seen; escaped from a high-security prison in a furniture van with a lift in it; on the run through Europe to Australia and then Brazil; kidnapped in a sack and ended up in Barbados; flown back to Brazil and his family there; and then travels back to the UK, his original starting point, after 40-plus years to be placed inside a high-security prison again. Guy Ritchie, this is a ready-made script for another blockbuster film. I can see Ray Winstone as Biggsy, Larry Lamb as Detective Jack Slipper ... My imagination could run riot, but on with the book.

These are the song lyrics for the tracks on the EP, which I can vouch for personally as giving a true account of events in Ronnie's life.

It's So Harsh in Belmarsh

Serving 28 years at seventy-three,
Come on, Mr Blunkett, set him free,
He won't harm you, he's an old man,
He escaped in a furniture van.
[CHORUS]
It's so harsh in Belmarsh.
It's so harsh in Belmarsh.
More than 30 years in Brazil,
He didn't rape, he didn't kill,
In '63 he robbed a train,
All the sorrow, all the pain.
[Chorus]
Michael's waiting by the prison gate,
We all know it's worth the wait,
He will never run away,
This is home, the glorious UK.
[Chorus]
His health is failing, he's near the end,
We all know this, let's not pretend,
Appeal Court judges in their wigs,
Please free Ronnie Biggs.

[Chorus - Repeat, Repeat and Fade]

This was to be the main A-side track and my aim was to make sure that there was no crossover or duplication of lyrics/themes. My second song was entitled '002731' and told another part of Ronnie Biggs's life, from his prison escape to being given the same prison number in 2001 as the one he had at Wandsworth in 1965.

002731

2001 Ronnie did land,
Loving son holding his hand,
Thirty-six years he has been away,
Glad to be back, he wouldn't say.
Down the stairs and into the van,
Is this all part of the plan?
Ronnie did say while under arrest,
"Oh my God, I'm a fucking pest."
[CHORUS]
He can't talk, he can only grunt,
Mr Blunkett, you fucking cunt.
[Repeat]
Twenty cop cars or maybe more,
Blacked-out windows with locks on the door.
He's been done up like a kipper,
He's being treated like the Yorkshire Ripper.
Straight to court and off to the nick,
Ronnie knows the Old Bill trick.
Open prison, you're having a laugh,
He was banged up without a bath.
[Chorus]
In and out of court for an Appeal,

Serving 28 years, is this for real?
"No," said the Judge, "you will not be free",
He robbed a train, not a killing spree.
Lying in the hospital wing,
Thinking of '63 just near Tring.
All his mates have shown support,
Grim shitty Belmarsh, it's like a fort.
[Chorus]
We all love you and the fight goes on,
We're it in till the end just for Ron.
[Chorus and Fade]

I e-mailed Frank so that he could see the lyrics for the first two songs, which I was happy to keep as they were. I just wanted him to confirm that his band could get their heads around the lyrics and produce a softer punk sound than their normal fast, hard-core delivery. The sound I was hoping they could achieve was something like The Sex Pistols, so that people could understand the words and appreciate their meaning, which was the whole point of producing this record.

Frank, being as fanatical as anyone where Ronnie was concerned, said that he would try to come up with some suitable music to accompany the lyrics and would then try them out with his band. In the meantime, I was working on the third song, which was entitled 'August 8th'. This song had a dual Biggsy meaning. Most importantly of all, the date was Ronnie Biggs's birthday, but it was also the anniversary date of the Great Train Robbery of 1963. Those of you that saw the 1988 comedy film *Buster* (as in Great Train Robber Buster Edwards, played by Phil Collins) will hopefully remember the scene when the money contained in hundreds of mailbags was being emptied onto the floor of the farm hideout, and one of the train robbers shouts out, "It's Harry's birthday", and then lights a rolled-up £50 pound note in celebration. Well, 'Harry' was Ronnie Biggs, who was 34 on the day of Britain's biggest ever robbery.

August 8th

Ronnie Biggs is seventy-four,
Why must he suffer anymore?
Every day he's in great pain,
Set him free once again.
[CHORUS]
Set him free.
His crime was over 40 years ago,
His reputation will always grow.
Ronnie was not the mastermind,
A replacement driver he had to find.
[Chorus]
The robbery happened on August eighth,
"I'm on your side," said the driver's mate.
Ronnie had it all to gain,
But he never set foot on the train.
[Chorus]
"Thirty years?" people did cry,
"For a robbery? Why, why, why?"
He was in Brazil for thirty years,
Ronnie didn't have any fears.
In Brazil he didn't break the law,
Jack Slipper did in '74.
[Chorus]
Lots of Appeals have been made,
They will not give us legal aid.
Rape a child, kill a fellow man,
You only get ten years in the can.
Thirty years for robbing a train,

It really is inhumane.

[Chorus]

The 'Free Ronnie Biggs' record now had three songs and I was creating a picture cover for it to make it more recognisable to the buyer and more eye-catching rather than just a plain white sleeve. Frank said he had a photograph that he'd taken in 2000 when he'd last visited Ronnie in Santa Theresa that would make a great picture for the front of the sleeve and, of course, no copyright issues would be involved if we used it. The photograph was of Ronnie standing in his backyard next to the swimming pool and wearing a black Rauschangriff T-shirt. Frank suggested superimposing the photo onto a Union Jack background, which sounded great. Before long we had conjured up so many ideas about the back cover and accumulated so much information - photographs, press cuttings or even lyrics - that we started to think that maybe we should consider a vinyl album to accommodate it all.

Images darted frantically between Epsom in Surrey and Munich, each e-mail opening up a newer version of the record cover. We both agreed on the front cover, so that was a goer, but the back cover was another issue entirely. We couldn't use newspaper headlines without facing copyright issues, so we mixed and matched the headlines of one paper with the story contained in another. We decided to use a large Brazilian flag as the background, together with a Ronnie Biggs fingerprint, and Frank added two of his favourite photographs (you bastard, Frank, I'm not in either one!): one of Michael and Ronnie laughing together in 1997 when the UK Government told the Brazilian authorities that it was no longer interested in extraditing Ronnie and that he was a free man so long as he stayed in Brazil; and the second one of Frank and the boys in his band Rauschangriff, which seemed only fair since they were the ones responsible for arranging the music, recording the tracks and sourcing a cheap record-pressing company. Obviously, having worked on such projects before, Frank already

84

had the right sorts of contacts and he found a pal in Romania who agreed to press 500 vinyl records with a picture cover and insert a lyrics sheet (A4 folded to A5), all for £300. This, Frank confirmed, was 'mates' rates' and so we scheduled a pressing/release date - 8 August!

As I was scribbling down the lyrics for song number four I was also getting the press release ready, which I gave the heading of: "Ronnie Biggs to be released on August 8th - the record, that is, not the legend". These were my actual words and why I was contacted by the Daily Mirror for an exclusive story (which I will tell you about later in this chapter).

I entitled my fourth song 'Daddy was a Train Robber'. I loved The Clash and especially reggae music, and when they released 'Bank Robber' I found it easy to substitute 'Train Robber' and alter the original lyrics sufficiently to cover my potentially copyright-whipped arse. Frank loved this song and his band played a wicked reggae riff. In fact it sounded so good in the studio that Frank was almost tempted to move it to the A side. However, we both agreed that this record was about Ronnie Biggs and not us, and that the Belmarsh name on the A-side title track said it all. After penning my 'Daddy was a Train Robber' lyrics, it struck me that it could be a great song for Michael Biggs and Nick Reynolds to sing together, as both their fathers were train robbers, but as it stood it was going to be a Rauschangriff number, not a duet. This latter idea would, however, come back to haunt me much sooner than I thought.

Daddy was a Train Robber
[CHORUS]
Daddy was a Train Robber, he never hurt nobody,
He just loved to live that way and loved to steal her money.
Bruce did say we'll all be rich,
Robbing a train without a hitch.
Two million quid left on the floor,

Get the hammer and smash the door.

[Chorus]

In the dead of night it was an awesome sight,
Postal workers observed with fright.
By three o'clock the train was bare,
The robbers gone to you know where.

[Chorus]

Time has passed and Ron's now home,
He's in prison by the Millennium Dome.
In Category A and that's not fair,
The prison staff they just don't care.

[Chorus]

Frank and the band were well into the recording of the four tracks now, and Frank said he wanted to add a final fifth track called 'King of the Punks', which was an old record of theirs from 1998 and it was about Ronnie, as Ron had recorded punk tracks with The Sex Pistols in 1978 and also with German pop/punk band Die Toten Hosen. Ronnie at the time loved the punk themes of rebellion and standing up to the authorities, and the Germans love to see our own people going against the grain, so to speak. Having heard Frank's song, I asked him if he would mind if I changed a few of the lyrics to give them that little 'English slang' twist, and when he recorded the revised lyrics he was overjoyed with it. Even now you can see Frank and the boys belting out all these songs on youtube.com. His English is superb, and what a memory.

King of the Punks

To me you're just a boring fart.
There's a man in Rio who's nearly seventy,
He's more a punk that you will ever be.

He's on the run from justice and law,

Scotland Yard came knocking on his door.

A prisoner of Rio he didn't like to be,

Better than 30 in their fucking HMP.

[CHORUS]

Ronnie, king of the punks.

Ronnie, last of the punks.

(Repeat)

He lived his life always on the run,

Lots of pain and lots of fun.

Who the hell is really innocent?

Cheers to the Brazilian government.

[Chorus - Repeat and Fade]

I was dying to hear the first demo of the EP, which was almost complete. The record cover designs had been finalised and we were two weeks away from the Romanian vinyl pressing date, which had been brought forward to 3 August to allow for shipping to the UK and other European destinations so it was available on the all-important 8 August date. On one side of the A4 lyric sheet were the words to all five songs and on the reverse was a photograph of Ronnie in his Brazilian football shirt, holding a copy of one of his books and underneath was with a four-paragraph story, detailing why we had produced the record and what we hoped to achieve with it. As mentioned earlier, also on the sheet was my 'Diary of a Sick Man', letting people know the torture and pain that Ronnie was enduring on a daily basis.

When the first CD demo arrived, I was very proud to hear my unchanged lyrics being pumped out by Frank's band. The music was pop-punk apart from 'Daddy was a Train Robber', which had a light reggae feel - although I would've wanted a more Mikey Dread/Clash feel to it given the choice. '002731' was superb - a slow ditty, with a vicious chorus of "He can't walk, he can only grunt/Mr Blunkett, you fucking cunt". I must admit I felt guilty writing those lyrics, Blunkett being blind and all, but he was responsible in my eyes for keeping Ronnie in Belmarsh and he made no bones about that. So the chorus was from me to you, David.

I had kept Michael Biggs informed of everything we were doing in terms of the record, as I did not want to upset him or his legal team by dropping this on their lap, especially if the tabloids took to the story as it could have backfired big time. Since the idea was born, I had teased Michael about him singing 'Daddy was ...', but he had laughed it off, because he said he would have to record it in Barnet, then post it to Frank for him to lay the vocals over the tracks, and all quality would be lost. So I suggested to Frank that Michael could visit Munich to record the song(s), if he had enough time, and we could fly him back the same day. Frank and I even agreed to pay Michael's airfare. To be fair, Frank sounded okay on the punk scene, but when you needed a UK audience to understand each and every lyric, it was a bit like Adolf Hitler singing a Frank Sinatra song! Sorry, Frank, but you know that now.

Michael said he would help us with the campaign record, and it only seemed right that he should be on lead vocals for 'Daddy was a Train Robber'. So Frank had to do it all again: studio/recording fees, etc. Michael also sang the background chorus on all the other tracks. Also it was a great weekend trip to Munich and cemented the bond between the Biggs family and Frank Werner.

Listening to the Demo 2 CD after the first Demo CD was like going from driving a Ford Mondeo to a BMW. Michael's voice was superb - well it should be, as he plays in a Brazilian band even today (2008) and he can be found most Sunday evenings in a Brazilian club in Covent Garden. Michael is a professional singer and has been since he was a small boy, playing in front of a recorded crowd of 100,000 people plus. I had to admire his enthusiasm for our record project, as no profit was to be made anywhere; just straightforward world awareness of his father's situation.

The Free Ronnie Biggs campaign PR person (me!) was kept very busy mailing all the UK media houses, newspapers, radio, television, music magazines, Internet sources, Yahoo news, youtube, My Space - you name it and a PR release was sent stating "Ronnie Biggs to be released on August 8th". The interest was phenomenal, although some critics did not agree because they did not read the second line: "The record, that is, not the legend". The *Daily Mirror* was the first to contact me, with the promise of a photograph of the record, quickly followed by *The Weekly News*, which has been on the go since I was a small boy. Both avenues seemed very promising. As an added bonus, I was contacted by a record company called Rough Trade, which was a legendary name during the early punk days of 1977 to 1979. So it was all looking very good.

The record was pressed and distributed as agreed - to me in the UK, Munich, Romania and Frank's pals in Russia and Croatia. We had already taken around 150 pre-pressed orders, some for single copies and others for ten-plus, and we had to make the £300 back that we had paid for out of our own pockets for the production costs. The total pressing number was 500 and they did look good. The quality of the colours and the printing made the record a very attractive item, although the lyric/information sheet was printed in black and white to reduce the costs.

I had my own record distribution list: the late John Peel; Sean at Rough Trade Records; journalists at national newspapers/magazines who over the years had actually printed what they said they would print, unlike the other journo bandits who wrote a totally different story and tried to make Ronnie and ourselves look stupid. Yes, you know who you are, because you keep returning for further exclusive stories, but you will not be getting them.

One of the journalists that had contacted me with a view to a story on the release of the single was Mr Yates at the *Daily Mirror*. He said that he genuinely sympathised with Ronnie Biggs and his current situation, so I mailed him a record. He was straight onto the phone saying that a story would be featured in the following day's *Daily Mirror*. I have to admit that I was a bit sceptical, as over the years *The Sun* had always been the Biggs paper, long before they brought Ronnie back in 2001. They always had Biggsy exclusives, such as the kidnap theory in 1981 and his release from Barbados with a massive headline: "Biggsy has done it again". God bless 'em. The *News of the World* couldn't get enough of Ronald Arthur Biggs either. They were the first to publish the story about Ronnie and The Sex Pistols back in 1978. The *Daily Mirror* story kick-started a wave of other local newspaper/radio station interest in the record and Ronnie's situation.

Another very charming person that I got to know over the Biggsy years was Robert Potter of the *Weekly News*. He was very approachable and always produced in his newspaper exactly what he had promised. He gave the record a full-page colour editorial, and on the opposite page was a feature on another of our Biggs supporters, Mr Uri Geller. Ronnie had known Uri since the Rio de Janeiro days and Uri was one of those people who took time out in 2001 to visit Ronnie in Queen Elizabeth Hospital when it looked as though we might lose him.

Over the following months all the records sold, apart from those that had been used as 'media gifts', which we had tried to keep to a minimum. In the end we covered our costs and made an additional £500 for the campaign, which we sent to Ronnie's legal team at the time, who were getting his case ready for an Appeal to the European Court of Human Rights. So our goal had been achieved. We had wanted to raise worldwide awareness of Ronnie's current health and the prison conditions, and we only had to look on Google to see that the story had spread as far afield as South Africa, Poland, Japan, Singapore, etc. As with all collectable records of this nature, the vinyl copies soon started appearing on eBay and our cover price of only five euros now had an eBay starting bid of 20 euros.

Midway through 2004 another Ronnie Biggs musical item was being advertised in the UK's music press: a CD remastered from 1974 and entitled *Mailbag Blues - The Ronnie Biggs Story*, which told the story of

Ronnie's life (prison escape, robbery, etc.) Ronnie had (and still has) such a strong love of jazz music that back in 1974 he got together with his friend Bruce Henri (US base player) and they composed the album together. The recording had lain hidden for years, and it wasn't until Ronnie's return to the UK in 2001 that Bruce digitally remastered the tracks and it was suddenly in record shops worldwide. The CD package includes a small booklet summarising Ronnie's life story, which features photos from the 1974 days. Bruce Henri said of the collaboration:

"*Mailbag Blues* was written over a couple months' period with Ronnie at our side telling us his story and us breaking it down into events that we most related to musically. The songs are structured as a soundtrack, each one telling us part of a story and leading on to the next. When we went into the studio to record, we had the whole album pretty well defined, but we left a lot of room for individual improvisation, as was the style in 1974.

"The recording took place in a very small room, on a four-track Ampex tape recorder. Everybody played together, and we only used playback on one or two tracks for additional percussion. We were so young and eager back then, and we took ourselves so seriously, that we wouldn't let Ronnie sing, which is too bad because he had a terrible voice but the Sex Pistols did all right with it didn't they?

"I met Ronnie Biggs as Mike Haynes, which was the name on his passport. At the time he was doing some carpentry work at my father's apartment, and was friends with Conti (Count Constantine Benckendorff who is married to my sister), who set up the whole *Daily Express* thing with Colin McKenzie (read *Odd Man Out* by Ronnie Biggs), so we all knew each other. After that fiasco when Biggs got arrested and then released from jail in Rio (after being 'nabbed' by Inspector Slipper, a.k.a. Slip-up), he had this idea to make a film with his story. He wanted to start by doing the soundtrack, his own soundtrack, with some of the musicians he admired. Now he could use his real name and, with a new project, he hoped to start a new life, in a new home with what resources (monetary and human) he had at the time. We talked about the album for about a month while we started putting some ideas together, then about two months to write the material, then recording took about a week. So in all it took around three to four months.

"It was definitely very rebellious music at the time, but not in a punk rock way. It was rebellious because nobody was making independent recordings back then, especially with no singer, and we were recording exactly what we wanted for the sake of the music, with no concern whatsoever with the marketing angle, for the simple reason that the marketing was the story itself. This was the soundtrack for a very exciting and unique life story, a great experience, an adventure that many people should feel envious of, people that never got the opportunity or never really had it in them to actually go out and stick one to the system. From my point of view, having always lived under dictatorships, from being brought up under Franco and then moving to Brazil just after the military coup, I was perpetually searching for ways to freely express myself and if possible simultaneously stick a finger at the government or the police (much the same thing in those days), or the political police if you prefer, without being nabbed.

"We were constantly renting venues to give 'underground' concerts and trying to show our 'new' music to a public without too much of a choice as far as jazz clubs and such go. I can't really even think of more than maybe one jazz club at the time, and the 'jazz' they played was something extremely polite and old fashioned, not something that 24-year-old musicians wanted to be playing. Ronnie went to our concerts, as did Mick Taylor and Jim Capaldi, but we weren't doing clubs. I used to go out and rent theatres and do my own production. This was more what would have been called 'progressive jazz'.

"To me Ronnie symbolised a rupture from the restraining chains of military dictatorships, politics, police, short hair and suits, and the overpowering right wing. He was a very interesting person to talk to, with a great story, and certainly a wonderful talent for story telling. I think Ronnie and I shared an attitude, in spite of his being some years older, he still had this adolescent restlessness in him, the adrenaline that drove him to do what he did in the first place, and similarly was looking for new forms of expression, a bit more tingle in his life, some glitter, some fun. For this reason, I guess we were the perfect match." (Bruce Henri, 2004)

Staying with the Ronnie Biggs musical theme, this year (2008) I again wanted to raise awareness of Ronnie's continuing position in Her Majesty's institutions, although now (July 2008) Ronnie is in HMP Norwich, a supposedly Category C prison, and I will tell you more about that in the next chapter. I wanted to jump on the youtube.com bandwagon, as I had seen that many Ronnie Biggs documentaries had been uploaded for viewing, but I didn't want a docudrama, I wanted images of Ronnie as he is today with music, so again I put on my John Lennon-esque songwriting head and began another exercise to let the public, Government or, in fact, anyone who would listen, know the facts, as I believe that Ronnie Biggs is knocking on heaven's door.

I wrote my own lyrics to the famous Bob Dylan song 'Knockin' on Heaven's Door' and my nephew Tom Thornton arranged the guitar and vocals, and I then added a four-minute photographic slide show, with pictures from Ronnie's 2001 UK return to the present day. To date, it has had over 3,700 viewings on youtube, so there are plenty of people who still care about Ronnie Biggs's welfare. It's a sad illustration of a lonely, harmless old man, still enduring the wrath of the British Government for a crime of robbery over 45 years ago.

Knockin' on Heaven's Door
by The Train Robberz (Mike Gray & Tom Thornton)

Take these handcuffs off of me,
I can't wear them any more.
I'm getting old, I cannot see,

I feel like I'm knockin' on heaven's door.

[CHORUS]

Knock knock knockin' on heaven's door.

(Repeat)

My life's a blur since '63,
I can't take it anymore.
'Political prisoner' they've labelled me,
I feel like I'm knockin' on heaven's door.

[Chorus]

My memories are a distant dream,
I was guilty but no more.
My life is not what it may seem,
I feel like I'm knockin' on heaven's door.

[Chorus]

Forgive me, Lord, and let me be,
My heart can't beat anymore.
Michael, my love is for thee,
I feel like I'm knockin' on heaven's door.

[Chorus – Repeat, Repeat and Fade)

Other bands have jumped on the Biggsy bandwagon over the years. German punk band Die Toten Hosen recorded several songs with Ronnie while he was in Brazil, and the lead singer of the band actually went to Ronnie's 70th birthday party in Rio in 1999. Their songs, such as 'Rio-Punk Was' and, one of my favourites, the old Clash hit 'Police on My Back', with Ronnie singing his heart out, can also be found on youtube. In 1981, when Ronnie was kidnapped, a vinyl record surfaced on the Virgin record label called 'Ronnie Biggs - He Was Only the Tea Boy'. All the royalties, as explained on the record cover, were being sent to the Johnny and Lia Pickston, the people looking after Michael Biggs. They have remained great friends to this day.

Over the years, Tel Currie has been a good pal of mine and, as explained earlier, he has always kept Roy Prettyboy Shaw's website up to date with the latest news about Ronnie's progress, as has Mick Gallagher on the Krays' website. In fact they've always given Ronnie pride of place on the sites' homepages, giving Ronnie's cause as much exposure as possible to everyone that logs on. Because of Tel's unswerving loyalty to Sir Ronnie, as Tel used to call him, I made a short youtube video entitled 'Tel Currie - Diamond Geezer', which shows Tel with all the underworld characters, past and present, that he knows. It has had over 2,000 hits, which gives you a clear idea of the respect he has from these guys. Thanks for all your support over the Belmarsh years, Tel, and I look forward to many more years being your true Pal. Respect.

Chapter 8
HMP Norwich and
the Fight Goes On
(by Mike Gray)

The third of July 2007 was a very memorable date for Ronald Arthur Biggs and everyone in the Free Ronnie Biggs campaign team. Ronnie had been told officially of his move from Belmarsh and on this date he was transferred to HMP Norwich. His 78th birthday was only a month away, so it was like getting an early birthday present, but after six years in high-security Belmarsh it hadn't come soon enough.

In an interview with the BBC, Ronnie's son Michael said that the transfer came out of the blue and that it was a victory for common sense, but he didn't think his father would ever be released. His words echoed what everyone thought: "My father can hardly walk, will never speak again and cannot eat or drink, or read and write - but he's still deemed to be a threat to society?" However, he was relieved that his father had been moved from a maximum secure prison and would be visiting him at Norwich over the coming weekend.

There had always been plenty of media speculation about Ronnie Biggs and if/when he might be released. One Sunday newspaper in October 2006 had put out the following story as factual:

'Free me and I'll go back to Brazil'
Great Train Robber Ronnie Biggs is launching a last-ditch bid for freedom
- by becoming a Brazilian citizen.
Biggs could be deported on a one-way ticket to Rio de Janeiro if his

request is granted by the Brazilian foreign ministry, his legal team claims.
The frail 77-year-old, who cannot walk or talk and is fed via a tube in
Belmarsh jail, would be freed under Brazilian law as his £2.3 million
crime was more than 40 years ago.

After escaping from Wandsworth prison in 1965 Biggs stayed in South
America for more than 30 years, wedding a local woman and having son
Michael.

His lawyer Giovanni di Stefano said officials in Brazil had told him Biggs
is eligible for citizenship.

Mr di Stefano said: "This avoids Home Secretary John Reid having to
make a decision about a sick, old man.

"It is Biggs's ticket to Rio and would allow him to die with his family
rather than in Belmarsh."

In December 2006, Tel Currie and I made headline news on the home
page of lawyer Giovanni di Stefano's website. Tel had e-mailed to ask if I
would approach Giovanni with a view to his representing lifer Charles
Bronson. Well, the rest is history, as Giovanni contacted Mr Bronson and
is currently battling for his freedom (August 2008). Tel was a very
important link in the Charlie Bronson campaign. Giovanni's story reads:

There is nothing more pleasant than to return back to Rome from the
Middle East and find a photo and card from a client, especially one as
nice as Charles Bronson. The more I study and look at his case the more
I am fully aware that to sentence this man to life was a drastic error. Just
appeared on my desk also is an e-mail from the actual victim who now
resides in Spain. He also seeks the release of Mr Bronson and cannot
understand or accept that a life sentence was imposed.

The case of Charles Bronson is and never can be a victory for me alone.
It is a victory for a whole movement and team. To name but a few: Mal,
Tel Currie, Mike Gray, Gary, Dave Courtney, the entire family of Charles

97

Bronson whom he loves, the countless who write and support, Jim Dawkins, and so many whom I have not had the pleasure of meeting that have worked endlessly far longer than myself to attain justice.

I have written to the Parole Board and the Chief Executive was kind enough to acknowledge the submissions, and if no proper action is taken I shall indeed pursue this to the hilt. The bases for imposing a life sentence in my view were not really met and it is a great shame that Lord Justice Rose did not have the courage to 'put a wrong right' as the imposing principles of the Court of Appeal. However, it has to be remembered that the Court of Appeal in England are known as gatekeepers not keepers of justice. They are often and far too frequently intellectually dishonest. The case of R v. Bronson is but one. But it is one that in reality cries out for review. Contrary to popular belief, the Court of Appeal can be so moved via an application to the Registrar. There are a number of cases that permit a review if the procedure has not been properly followed or if the Court of Appeal have acted upon erroneous information. The case of R v. Porter is but one. There are others. I have been able to take the case of John 'Goldfinger' Palmer back to the Court of Appeal. Biggs was refused even though I proved he was not present at the appeal hearings when the case was called. The case of Bronson is one that there is a chance may well have to be reviewed via the Registrar or the CCRC. What is certain is that Bronson should not be subjected to any further terms of custody. The reality of the matter is not that he deserves to be in jail but that the 'system' knows not what to do or what risk he poses. The answer to that question is that we shall never know unless he is released and since his record is not one with what I would term serious offences, namely murder or manslaughter, but only an intolerance for what Mr Bronson considers unacceptable behaviour and for years he has not committed an act of violence, so it seems to me that his continued custody is solely upon his reputation.

Now we have to remember that when the Train Robbers were at large the then Chief Constable gave a press statement that members of the public should not approach them as he feared they may even have 'nuclear capacity weapons'. So you can see simply how absurd and stupid the system actually is and far more so than what the system fears of Mr Bronson. Now we must remember that when the Chief Constable made that statement regarding the Train Robbers the Cuban Missile Crisis was only a couple of years old!!!!

The release of Mr Bronson is an important issue for the sake of fairness, equity and jurisprudence. He has a place to reside and many, many, many friends. Even the victim for which the life sentence was imposed supports him! Why has he remained in jail for so long? Not because he is a danger but that he is considered to 'maybe be a danger', which actually can fit anyone in the UK right now. But the victory for Mr Bronson will be a victory for ALL that have campaigned and I have a couple of aces up my sleeve yet ... (Giovanni di Stefano, 7 December 2006)

On Christmas Eve, Giovanni followed up this statement with 'A Message to the World' regarding Ronnie Biggs and Charlie Bronson:

Charles Bronson and Ronnie Biggs remain in prison because of the bigot of a Home Secretary who cannot see further than his nose. Actually it is probably not even John Reid. Most times when applications/letters/petitions are addressed to him he does not even read them. It's some pen-pusher men in grey who hide in corridors at Queen Anne's Gate at the Home Office. Blast those that have no heart. No heart to see that Ronnie Biggs is dying and needs his family. Blast those bigots that have targeted Charles Bronson simply because they don't like the way he looks, the way he talks, the way he moves and thus keep him in prison for no other reason. (Giovanni di Stefano, 24 December 2006)

And then, on the anniversary of Ronnie's sentencing in 1964, Giovanni made another statement:

On the 16th April 1964 Ronald Biggs received 30 years' imprisonment for being a participant in what is known as the Great Train Robbery. The judge at Buckinghamshire Assizes in Aylesbury, Mr Justice Edmund Davies, said it would be "positively evil" if he showed leniency.

Biggs subsequently escaped from prison, eventually ended up in Brazil and despite a number of attempts to extradite him (all failed) and a kidnapping (also failed) his return to the UK was voluntary. In fact on the 7th May 2001 he returned to prison and to this day has lived in an almost vegetative state. Here is his photo. In 2005 I asked the Home Secretary to release him on compassionate grounds. Despite having received indications that an affirmative reply would be received he was refused. I applied again twice in 2006 and again was refused. I am applying again. In effect from the 30-year sentence Biggs had served nearly 2 years from the day of his arrest (pre trial) to the day he 'escaped' on the 8th July 1965. From the day he returned voluntarily in 2001 to date he has served a further six years. That is eight years total imprisonment. Those that think he had easy street life in Brazil can think again. I have spoken with Mr Biggs and his family. But he has now served 8 years of an excessive 30-year sentence and he is old, infirm, cannot walk, cannot talk, cannot go to the toilet, and is in constant need of medical care. If he had not escaped and had the old parole system been in place in 1974 he would invariably have been released because in those days (actually not that long ago) one was released on parole after one-third of the sentence.

I found a serious fault in his trial and more important his appeal. He was NOT PRESENT during the actual appeal. The UK Courts work on what is called judicial precedent. That means that the law constantly develops and when an appeal court gives a judgement contained within the judgement are reasons. In a case called PORTER it was decided, and in fact is embossed in stone, that if an appellant is not present in the courtroom (unless he waives the right to be present) the hearing is null and void. The case of Porter was about a lorry driver who actually killed a few people because he was so tired driving that he fell asleep. The Trial Court gave him 5 years imprisonment for three lives. He appealed. It was as you would expect dismissed. BUT Mr Porter was only in the cells of the Royal Courts of Justice and not in Court. His lawyers wrote to the Registrar and the Registrar (a great man called Mike Mackenzie-boy, how I miss him) with spirit, firmness and fairness of mind, referred the case to the court again. His sentence was reduced to 4 years. Now Biggs found himself in 1965 in the same position. He was in the cells, I proved that, and obtained an affidavit, but the new Registrar instead of applying judicial precedent took my letter to Lord Justice Rose who would not even permit a re-sentence hearing. If Biggs had killed Mr Mills the train engineer maybe he would have been out by now! Mr Porter killed 3 people and received a reduced sentence because he was in the cells of the RCJ and not the Courtroom. Biggs was not permitted a re-hearing.

I have thus written today on the anniversary of sentence to the Lord Chief Justice to use the powers vested in him to at the least let us go back to court and hear the sentence appeal. It matters not the result but it's the fairness that counts. Why should Porter have a new appeal hearing and not Biggs? Because Biggs's sentence was political whilst Porter was causing death by dangerous driving? I am cautiously expecting from the Lord Chief Justice some justice and those of the media I expect support. (Giovanni di Stefano, 16 April 2007)

It was only a week after this statement that *The Sunday People* reported that Ronnie would be free in three years' time:

> *'Biggs Will Stay in Jail Until 2010' (by Nick Pisa)*
>
> *GREAT Train Robber Ronnie Biggs has been told he will freed in THREE years.*
>
> *But his lawyer believes the frail 77-year-old crook has only months to live anyway.*
>
> *Giovanni Di Stefano, launching a new appeal for Biggs's release, said it was "positively evil" keeping him in the hospital wing at Belmarsh jail, south-east London.*
>
> *Speaking of the 2010 release date, he said: "I'm very grateful to the Home Office for giving us this concession.*
>
> *"But it's very likely Ronnie Biggs will die in jail long before that.*
>
> *"He cannot walk, talk, eat or go to the toilet. He is in a vegetative state.*
>
> *"It's unlikely he will live for more than a few months. I'd like to help him die outside jail."*
>
> *Biggs, originally given 30 years, returned to Britain in 2001 after 35 years on the run. Two previous appeals for early release have failed.*

According to media reports, the Governor of HMP Norwich has refused to comment on Ronnie, saying that the Home Office does not discuss individual prisoners' cases. However, now that Ronnie had become Norwich's most infamous inmate (their previous media-magnet prisoner being Reggie Kray), it was obvious that he would be giving the prison a much higher profile than usual.

Michael called me on 4 July 2007, the day after his transfer to Norwich, to confirm that he had been called by the Home Office and had received a explanation for Ronnie's transfer as well as confirmation that he could visit and various details about the prison itself. He was told that HMP Norwich was a Category C prison with its own Healthcare Centre, which was situated in the outer prison (outside the main walls of HMP Norwich), along with the Young Offenders facility. It all sounded good and it set our minds on Ronnie's eventual release.

I telephoned Tel Currie, to pass on the information I had received from Michael Biggs, and we discussed the transfer in detail. Was it a good move? Why did they choose Norwich? How difficult would a visit be? How long would he be there?

Visiting times to see Ronnie in the Healthcare Unit are on Tuesdays or Sundays, from 2 p.m. until 4 p.m., although visits used to be for just one hour and the times have only recently been extended (mid-2008). The Unit contains 28 beds and there is 24-hour nursing cover, with weekly visits from a dentist, and optician and chiropody services available on a monthly basis. As Tel and I weren't family, we were only allowed to visit once a month.

When I visited Ronnie for the first time in HMP Norwich, I couldn't help but notice how serene the atmosphere was in and around the prison. The building is set on the top of a hill overlooking the beautiful city of Norwich. On entering Knox Road, a very long narrow road that runs straight to the prison's main gate, I noticed a pub (The Windmill) halfway down the road, with not another building in sight. As German Frank, who had flown over from Munich to visit Ronnie, and I had arrived a bit early we grabbed a quick lunch in the pub, which surprisingly enough was full of prison officers with sandwiches and a pint, mixing freely with regulars and visitors. Also there were some of the Visiting Centre staff, who were so polite and friendly in comparison to the awkward and difficult booking-in staff at Belmarsh.

Already I was getting a feel-good factor about this place. Only two security checks were made on entering the prison. There was no hand stamping or inserting fingers into an electronic imager, just a check of your ID with photograph and then a brief body search and introduction to the sniffer dog. Then you were politely invited into the small Healthcare

Centre visiting hall, which resembled an extended Scout hut with a snack bar. Unlike at Belmarsh (again), as we entered the hall the legend himself was sat in his wheelchair awaiting our arrival. Okay, our seats were still bolted to the floor, but we could move around freely, mess about with Ronnie and have a laugh without shouts of "Sit down! Where are you going? Don't move that!" etc. Yes, Mister Senior Officer with the beard in HMP Belmarsh (Ronnie knows who I'm talking about, as he took great pleasure in pointing the officer out to me every time I visited him), I dislike you as much as you obviously disliked me.

HMP Norwich actually received some very bad publicity in 2005. An inspection report in August of that year (posted on the Prison Reform Trust website) criticised certain aspects of the accommodation and healthcare, deeming them "unfit for habitation" and highlighting lapses in safety procedures, despite recent deaths at the prison, and also failures in the provision of vocational education in what is essentially a training prison. A key issue highlighted was the lack of suicide awareness training for staff and serious deficiencies in the whole system of care and support for vulnerable prisoners. Even the conditions in Healthcare Unit where Ronnie is housed came under criticism. Many cells were described as cold and dirty, and overcrowding (e.g. three prisoners squeezed into a cell designed to accommodate just one) was also a major issue. This was only the latest in a line of reports to uncover shocking conditions in the UK's prisons. Treating prisoners with such lack of decency and failing to train or educate them is wrong and hugely inhibits the success of their resettlement in the community. More and more people are being sent to prison for non-violent, non-serious offences, and the consequent overcrowding is the root cause of many of the problems and compromises the safety of the prisoners. HMP Norwich has a certified accommodation figure of 591, but population counts in 2005 revealed that prisoner numbers were 180 higher than this.

The national newspapers and TV media only seemed to be displaying one message: "Biggs moved to Soft Prison". Well, in view of the damning report three years ago, the label of 'soft' doesn't really seem to fit. To be honest, although Ronnie is now in a lower-security Category C prison, it isn't a lot different from HMP Belmarsh. He still has a high prison wall around him and cannot be pushed around the prison grounds in his wheelchair as we all had all hoped. We all wanted and expected an open prison, but the Home Office said that he had been transferred to Norwich because of the healthcare facilities there. If that's the truth and they can prolong his life, then I agree it's a good move, but if couldn't Ronnie have been looked after in an open prison, just having his feeding tube cleaned and taking his tablets, etc.? I think that placing him in an open prison might have opened the floodgates for every Tom, Dick and Harry in the UK media wanting to stroll around with Biggsy and the authorities didn't want that sort of media circus around him. Oh well, who knows? I guess we should be thankful for small mercies, and getting Ronnie out of 'Hellmarsh' was a mercy in itself.

My letter to Giovanni di Stefano on 4 July 2007 made the headlines on his website:

Michael Biggs called me yesterday to say the Home Office had contacted him, and it would not be made public until this morning (Wednesday 4 July). And the story is already in The Daily Mirror.

This is absolutely great news for Ronnie, Michael and myself and all connected to the Free Ronnie Biggs campaign, as we have never given up on Ron and maintained a high-profile campaign, by writing to Her Majesty the Queen, numerous Home Secretaries, etc. As a regular visitor to Belmarsh to see Ron, I can fully understand when Michael told me yesterday that Ronnie was "crying" with excitement.

I would personally like to thank Giovanni di Stefano for his efforts in getting Ronnie moved. God bless that man.

Thank you once again to ALL OF YOU who have, over the past 6 years, supported Ronnie, written to him, visited him on a regular basis (yes, Tel and Roy, I mean you two) and anyone who is supporting our cause ... THANK YOU.

Norwich Prison (Healthcare Wing) is where Reggie Kray spent some time on 28th July 2000. How ironic that Biggsy has gone to the same Healthcare Wing in the month of July. Ronnie is 78 years old on 8th August.

Should you wish to write to Ronnie and welcome him to his NEW HOME, the details are:

RONALD ARTHUR BIGGS, PRISONER 002731, HMP NORWICH, KNOX ROAD,

NORWICH, NR1 4LU

Thank you and RESPECT to you all, Mike.

Mike Gray

Organiser, Free Ronnie Biggs Campaign

Giovanni di Stefano is continuing to fight Ronnie's corner and secure his release, and on 3 August 2007 he wrote the following comprehensive letter to plead his case once again:

Mr James Hough,

Release & Recall Section,

Directorate of the National Offender Manager,

Room 135 Abell House,

John Islip Street,

London, SW1P 4LH

Cc: Ministry of Justice,

The Rt. Hon. Mr Jack Straw,

Selborne House,

54 Victoria Street,

London, SW1E 6QW

Dear Sir,

Re: Ronald Arthur BIGGS

As you will be aware in October of 2005 our agents in the United Kingdom Messrs Paul Martin & Co were informed it was the decision of the Secretary of State for the Home Department not to release the above on compassionate grounds. We continue to represent and advise Mr. Biggs and kindly request all communication and correspondence is with us direct. In 2006 we made a further application which was also refused although the grounds upon which such were refused seemed unclear.

On the instructions of our client we left the matter for a period of time in order that the Home Office would re-asses the situation and we have further awaited for the Home Office to be effectively divided into the Home Office and Ministry for Justice.

Our client has thus received no reviews for what amounts to two years. We thus re-apply for release notwithstanding that in a positive manner our client was indeed transferred from HMP Belmarsh to HMP Norwich. Our client has fully appreciated this move but we are instructed to state that the said transfer cannot for one moment compensate the need and urgency for our client to spend his remaining period of life with his family for compassionate reasons.

You will be aware that another of our previous clients ETHEL ANN TRIGWELL serving a life sentence with a tariff of twenty years was in April released on compassionate grounds owing to her terminal illness. Mercifully she remains alive and will spend her remaining time in freedom. Our client Mr. Biggs will on the 8th August 2007 be 78 years of age and as you will be well aware the quality of his life for the past six years has been anything but to be considered positive. In short he cannot walk, talk, eat, perform ablutions, read, without assistance. His period in HMP Belmarsh in our view is to be considered as having served his full term of imprisonment. He has not been able to de facto perform the normal human functions for years and there was a period, supported by your own medical reports, which predicted his life expectancy far shorter than that predicted for ETHEL ANN TRIGWELL.

We do not wish to seem ungrateful for the act of compassion exhibited by the Government for Ms Trigwell or in fact for any other serving inmate under such tragic circumstances but we do wish to draw your attention to the fact that our client Ronald Biggs is worthy of a compassionate release and should be considered for such urgently.

It 2005 and 2006 it was made clear by the Secretary of State that the matter regarding Ronald Biggs and compassionate release would receive further consideration in 'due course' and that such compassionate release would be reviewed regularly. Neither we nor our agents have received any notification of any review in the past twelve months.

We briefly recant the facts of the matter as below and ask that you accept this letter as a formal application under S.36(1) of the Criminal Justice Act 1991 for compassionate release of Mr. Biggs:

Introduction

1. Mr. Ronald Arthur Biggs was convicted on 14th April 1964 for his part in the 'Great Train Robbery'. He was sentenced to a total of 30 years imprisonment.

2. In 1964, some months into his sentence, Mr. Biggs escaped from HMP Wandsworth and left the jurisdiction, eventually settling in Brazil. Following years of unsuccessful attempts by the British Government to secure Mr. Biggs' return by extradition, Mr. Biggs voluntarily returned to the jurisdiction on 3rd May 2001, and to his unexpired sentence. He is currently being held at the hospital department of HMP Belmarsh.

3. Mr. Biggs is a 77-year-old man of very poor health. Under cover of a letter dated 15th June 2005, we made an application under Section

36(1) of the Criminal Justice Act 1991 for Mr. Biggs' release on compassionate grounds.

4. The application was rejected by the Secretary of State for the Home Department on 26th October 2005.

5. The application set out the background facts, including the eventual sentences imposed on Mr. Biggs' co-defendants. The application set out Mr. Biggs' lack of risk of re-offending, his frail medical condition and his communication difficulties and requested that he be released to the care of his son.

Merits

6. The framework under which such an application should be determined is contained in Prison Service Order (PSO) 6000 issued on 31st March 2005 which deals with parole, release and recall of prisoners. Chapter 12 sets out the criteria for early release on compassionate grounds ('ERCG').

7. It is clear from paragraph 12.4 of PSO 6000 that the application was properly made and that the Secretary of State has the power to order release on compassionate grounds:

"12.4.1 Early release may be considered where a prisoner is suffering from a terminal illness and death is likely to occur soon. There are no set time limits, but three months may be considered to be an appropriate period. It is therefore essential to try to obtain a clear medical opinion on the likely life expectancy. The Secretary of State will also need to be satisfied that the risk of re-offending is past and that there are adequate arrangements for the prisoner's care and treatment outside prison.

12.4.2 Early release may also be considered where the prisoner is bedridden or severely incapacitated. This might include those confined to wheelchairs, paralysed or severe stroke victims. Applications may also be considered if further imprisonment would endanger the prisoner's life or reduce his or her life expectancy. Conditions which are self-induced, for example following a hunger strike, would not normally qualify a prisoner for release."

8. The general principles applicable to ERCG are set out in paragraph 12.3, that

"12.3.1 (i) the release of the prisoner will not put the safety of the public at risk;

(ii) a decision to approve release would not normally be made on the basis of facts of which the sentencing or appeal court was aware;

(iii) there is some specific purpose to be served by early release."

9. The relevant specific criteria to be applied to an ERCG application are set out in Appendix A to PSO 6000 and are as follows:

"(i) Medical

- the prisoner is suffering from a terminal illness and death is likely to occur soon; or the prisoner is bedridden or similarly incapacitated; and
- the risk of re-offending is past; and
- there are adequate arrangements for the prisoner's care and treatment outside prison; and
- early release will bring some significant benefit to the prisoner or his/her family.

(iii) General

The following factors need also to be considered:

- whether temporary release under the Prison Rules could significantly reduce the prisoner's and/or family's suffering;
- the length of the sentence still outstanding; the effect on the overall sentence passed by the court if early release is granted; and any remarks which the trial judge made on sentencing which may have a bearing on the question of release;
- the wishes of the prisoner and his/her family and the level of benefit which would derive to the prisoner and/or the family from permanent release;
- in medical cases, the diagnosis and prognosis; in particular whether

there is a specific estimate of life expectancy; and the degree of incapacitation.

In addition the Secretary of State may release a prisoner if he is satisfied that other exceptional circumstances exist."

10. Those conditions precedent were clearly met as was evidenced in the reports submitted.

11. There is and remains extensive medical evidence available from no less than four doctors. The Secretary of State also benefited from careful, detailed and thorough grounds and arguments advanced on Mr. Biggs's behalf by us confirming the criteria for such an application having been met.

12. Mr. Biggs's medical condition was considered 'stable'. The determination, based on the proper material and considerations, was that there was 'adequate treatment and care in prison'. Mr. Biggs does in fact have a permanent helper.

13. However, it can never be the case that simply because medical conditions in prison appear to be more apt in these circumstances than those offered by the NHS be justified as a reason for refusing an application.

14. The basis and ratio behind the decision not to release Mr. Biggs in October 2005 was in fact that the Prison facilities were 'better' than those that were available by the NHS and that Mr. Biggs's son did not make available or could not make available the 24-hour care required and as supplied by the Prison Service. The application was thus rejected in October 2005.

It is of course correct that in October 2005 we could have applied to the Administrative Court to review the decision of the then Secretary of State. However, we chose to allow a suitable passage of time and circumstances upon which any application would be based.

It is clear from the medical reports then available that Mr. Biggs's health was less than poor. Life expectancy could not be estimated and mercifully

Mr. Biggs has still remained in life to date.

However, in accordance with the guidelines a period of more than twelve months has now elapsed and whilst the guidelines clearly indicate that reviews on a three-monthly basis are appropriate we have allowed the now Minister of Justice further time. We have also considered the question of the public feeling in the matter. We have asked the question as to whether the release of Mr. Biggs would provoke a public outcry and diminish confidence in the criminal justice system. The Minister of Justice will know that a number of British and Foreign News Media have all supported the call for Mr. Biggs to be granted compassionate release. We can also confirm that we have now nearly 7,000 letters from individuals supporting a petition to HM the Queen for the prerogative of pardon to be issued.

We would, however, at this stage kindly request on behalf of Mr. Biggs that the Minister of Justice orders compassionate release in accordance with the criteria, which have been met, and in compliance with S.36(1) of the Criminal Justice Act 1991.

We also wish to make clear we are only concerned with the well being and care of Mr. Biggs and for his wish, supported by his family, and many others for Mr. Biggs to spend his remaining days with his family. The then Secretary of State, when making his decision in October 2005, invariably relied upon the public conception that any decision releasing a convicted offender into the community on such a high-profile case may have repercussions especially as it was considered that the health care available to Mr. Biggs at HMP Belmarsh could not be matched by the NHS. We feel, however, to be addressed the only issue outstanding is for the NHS to simply find a nursing home close to the family of Mr. Biggs whereupon Mr. Biggs may reside upon release. In the alternative, Mr. Biggs can be well cared for by his son Michael Biggs who is a British citizen, is resident in the United Kingdom, and who frankly has devoted his entire life to be near his father surrendering an excellent career in

Brazil for the sake of his father. Michael Biggs has stated to us that his love and devotion to his father remain the most important part of his life bearing in mind that from birth Michael was cared for by our client and raised as an honest citizen.

Finally, we kindly request a speedy decision in this matter, taking into account the condition, frailty and age of Mr. Biggs. It would be nothing short of a tragedy if Mr. Biggs were to die in custody. We thus request the immediate application of compassionate release, our client clearly meeting the criteria.

We thank you in advance for your kind consideration.

Yours sincerely
STUDIO LEGALE INTERNAZIONALE
Giovanni Di Stefano
Cc: The Rt. Hon. Mr Jack Straw

On Ronnie's birthday a few days later, the following was uploaded onto Giovanni's website:

Today is the birthday of Ronald Biggs. I have no idea what the Minister of Justice is playing at in keeping him in prison still, but it is high time that he grabbed the bull by the horns and made a proper decision to simply let him out and live his days with his family. I have received support from 23 different countries' media from Australia, Canada, Brazil and even China. Reports of my application for his release have grabbed the attention of the world media. Why? Because it has merit! Will the real Jack Straw please stand up and release Ronald Biggs immediately?! I urge as many as possible to sign my petition on the home site of my firm's website or write to me in support of the release of Ronald Biggs at the addresses on our contact page. HAPPY BIRTHDAY RONNIE! (Giovanni di Stefano, 8 August 2007)

Two further updates appeared on Giovanni's website in the following month, the first with news in response to his letter to the Ministry of Justice:

I am PLEASED to confirm that subsequent to my letter to the Minister of Justice The Rt. Hon. Mr Jack Straw QC the said Minister has decided to call for new reports on my client Ronald Biggs with a view to compassionate release. The new medical reports will be made available to me shortly and a decision taken subsequent. I am hopeful of a positive outcome which will permit Mr. Biggs to live his remaining time with his family. (Giovanni di Stefano, 11 September 2007)

So things were looking promising. I am in regular e-mail contact with Giovanni and I thank God that he took on the Ronnie Biggs case years ago, otherwise I can only assume that Ronnie would still be in Belmarsh with no transfer on the horizon whatsoever. He has always kept me updated on any movements with Ronnie's case, and his website is always bang up-to-date with information, and the details about the case are superb, accurate and honest.

Giovanni's respect for the Biggs family and his confidence that a release date for Ronnie is on the horizon are illustrated in the following extract from his website:

Mike Biggs is the extremely loyal son of Ronnie Biggs and I think that this time we may succeed in reuniting them. Remember it was Ronnie that actually raised Mike and as a unique son Mike has remained in Britain to be near his father. I have considerable admiration for Mike Biggs. Now most will know that Mike Biggs was in Brazil by far MORE famous than his father. He was part of a boy pop group called Balao Magico and he sold more than 12 MILLION records with a number of songs. One of those songs was PUPPY LOVE in Portuguese called CORACAO DE

PAPELAO which roughly translated means cardboard heart. Here is a picture of Mike's group. Now what we are going to do is to RE-RECORD PUPPY LOVE and release the single on the day (I hope or as soon as...) Jack Straw MP grants Ronnie Biggs compassionate release.

So even I from this far away land I have been able to re-write the music to PUPPY LOVE as an MP3 and have sent it both to Mike Biggs and JustCarmen and with the words. Mike Biggs will sing some in Portuguese and JustCarmen some in English as a duet. It will be recorded in Rome and SOONER than you all think. Why Puppy Love and not another song? It's a great catchy tune. One that you can easily whistle. Written by that great maestro Paul Anka and sung by Donny Osmond and a host of others. The version that celebrates the day of freedom for Ronnie Biggs will be one to remember. Now JustCarmen of course works with me as her producer and knows how difficult I can be and there are some awful rows as Dec Cluskey of The Batchelors can verify. But I think this recording with Mike and JustCarmen will be easy. After all, it's a celebration so we must all let our hair down a little ... well, what little I have left ... (Giovanni di Stefano, 12 September 2007)

I cannot thank Giovanni enough for his tireless work and effort regarding Ronnie, and whenever we discuss Giovanni at visits he gets the famous Biggsy thumbs-up - and, trust me, not many people get that from Biggsy.

As a result of the many high-profile cases that Giovanni has taken on, involving notorious clients, he has earned the media nickname of 'The Devil's Advocate', but as far as Ronnie's friends and family are concerned, he has been nothing but honest and decent and we back him 100%. Should you wish to know more about Giovanni or read up-to-date reports about Ronnie or his other big cases, please visit his website at **www.studiolegaleinternazionale.com.**

In early October, Giovanni was once again hot on the heels of the powers that be and applying the necessary pressure to secure Ronnie's release on compassionate grounds:

3 October 2007

Mr. James Hough,
Release & Recall Section,
Directorate of the National Offender Manager,
Room 135 Abell House,
John Islip Street,
London, SW1P 4LH
Cc: Ministry of Justice
The Rt. Hon. Mr Jack Straw

Dear Sir,

Re: Ronald Arthur BIGGS

We refer to our letter of 3rd August 2007 and your subsequent reply stating that medical reports were ordered and commissioned and we could expect copies shortly. It is now October and we would be obliged if you would confirm WHEN we can expect these and a formal decision. BUPA has agreed in principle to accommodate Mr Biggs if he is released on compassionate grounds and not a serving inmate and we take the view that this must satisfy at least one concern for the Ministry of Justice. In the past month we have received over 1,000 letters from the general public supporting the release of Mr Biggs and you will no doubt be aware that in a recent Daily Mail Poll, notwithstanding an absurdly negative article published, 56% of those polled were in favour of Mr Biggs' compassionate release against 44% contrary.

Whilst opinion polls should not per se make much of a difference to any decision taken by the Ministry of Justice, we cannot but comment that the said Ministry is the custodian of those who transgress the law for and on behalf of the citizens of England & Wales and as such their views may thus be considered.

We would be obliged if you would let us know as soon as possible regarding the release of Mr Biggs on compassionate grounds, who certainly in our submission is worthy of such mercy and grace.

We thank you in advance for your kind consideration.

Yours sincerely
STUDIO LEGALE INTERNAZIONALE
Cc The Rt. Hon. Mr Jack Straw

On the same date as Giovanni's letter, a newspaper reported that Ronnie had been offered a place in a retirement home - at Hadley Lawns Residential and Nursing Home in Barnet, Herts. - very close to where his son Michael lives, so it appeared that BUPA had done their bit and a compassionate release was getting closer. However, there were also media stories suggesting that Ronnie would live in Brazil on his release, well away from the media spotlight, and a statement from Giovanni Di Stefano on behalf of Ronnie Biggs confirmed that such a move could indeed be on the cards:

Mr Biggs received a visit yesterday 3rd October 2007 at HMP Norwich where he is currently being held.

In order to facilitate the release of Mr Biggs I can make the following promises to the appropriate authority.

I can confirm Mr Biggs on his release wishes to reside outside the United Kingdom. I have spoken with the Brazilian Ministry of Foreign Affairs who have confirmed that Mr Biggs may re-enter Brazil at anytime as during his 37 years in the country he lived a law abiding life committing no crimes and accused on no crimes.

He will, also, on his release refuse any inducement to speak to the media, other than issue a statement denouncing his actions in relation to the Great Train Robbery.

Mr Biggs states the following:

"There is no honour to be known as a Great Train   Robber. I regret my actions, and I apologise for glamourising what should only be thought of as a wilful crime. Before my death, I wish to deter those who may think of following a criminal way of life.

"My life has been wasted, and as I reflect on my years as a fugitive, I accept that cocking a snook at the police was a mistake during my time in Brazil. I acted like a child and can only apologise belatedly for my behaviour.

"If I can make some amends by urging others not to follow my lead, nor benefit financially from my criminal deeds for the rest of my life, then I will die happy. All I ask is to live the remainder of my days as a free man, to enjoy a peace and tranquillity I have denied myself.

"Crime does not pay - as I have proved."

Upon the release of Mr Biggs, news editors and photo journalists will be able to take photographs and see for themselves that his statement, "All I ask is to live the remainder of my days as a free man, to enjoy a peace and tranquillity I have denied myself. Crime does not pay - as I have proved," will be evident.

It is Mr Biggs' desire to return to Brazil and to spend his days with his family. I have received in the past month over 2,000 individual letters and 7,000 signatures on the petition to use compassion and release Mr Biggs. The letters emanate from police officers, retired Customs and Excise officers, teachers, doctors, factory workers, from all spheres of life in the United Kingdom. I call upon the Minister of Justice to free Mr Biggs

on compassionate grounds as he fulfils the criteria required for such
release. (Giovanni di Stefano, 3 October 2007)

A couple of weeks later, Giovanni di Stefano clarified a post he had made
the previous month on his website in which he had hinted at who had
given the Great Train Robbery gang the nod about the unusually large
amount of cash the train would be carrying on that particular night. Had
the information, which was known to the prosecuting authorities, been
revealed to the Defence at the time of Ronnie's trial it could have had an
impact on Ronnie's sentence:

Reginald Bevins, at that time Postmaster General, issued a statement that
the Robbery was "an inside job" and declared a public enquiry. That
enquiry took place but it was not a public but private enquiry. The report
was suppressed because it named the 'suspected person' who gave
information. That report was never made available to the Defence of any
of the so-called Great Train Robbers, let alone Ronald Biggs. That report
was further suppressed in 1968 and only one copy remains. It was
suppressed by the new Postmaster General in person JOHN
STONEHOUSE (God Rest His Soul) because it was HE, JOHN
STONEHOUSE, that was named as the 'suspected person' giving
information to a third party, a lawyer from Birmingham (not prosecuted),
who in turn referred the information to a member of the 'gang'.
The Prosecuting Authorities knew that when Biggs et al were prosecuted
but failed to inform, as was their duty, the Defence. It may well NOT have
made any difference regarding conviction BUT may have had an effect
upon sentence.
The fate of John Stonehouse is a matter of public record. He received a
part of the proceeds of the Great Train Robbery and with such he
pursued his business interests and the law of silence was maintained by
the Great Train Robbers. Until now ...

Throughout the latter parts of 2007, continued requests from Giovanni and his legal team seemed to fall on deaf Home Office ears. The regular visits to see Ronnie made by Tel, German Frank and I seemed to become easier in terms of the travelling, which involved a journey from London's Liverpool Street to Norwich via either Ipswich or Cambridge, depending on whether the overhead cables were knackered at some point in Essex - usually Chelmsford, which would totally fuck up the outward journey as it meant a 20-minute uphill walk to the prison. However, always getting the earlier train seemed to pay off for us, and the walk back to the station after the visit was more relaxed and, of course, downhill.

Giovanni was very busy during December 2007. Rumours were flying around about his request to the Home Office to allow Ronnie's custodial terms while being held in Brazil and Barbados to be included with his UK custody term. He again sent submissions to Jack Straw for Ronnie's release:

8 December 2007

GDS/DM/SM/BIGGS07

The Rt. Hon. Mr Jack Straw PM c/o

J. Hough, Esq.,

National Offenders Management Section,

Pre Release Section

4th Floor, Fry Building,

2 Marsham Street,

London, SW1P 4DF

Dear Mr. Hough,

Re: Ronald BIGGS - Early Release on Compassionate Grounds

I refer to your letter of the 31st October and the Medical Report that you duly attached. Would you please accept our kind and sincere apologies for any delay in replying, but we have taken advice on the matter in general.

We are of course grateful for the Medical Reports and the care that Mr. Biggs is receiving at HMP Norwich. We note that, according to the medical evidence, there is a slight improvement to his condition and certainly, considering the manner in which he was treated at HMP Belmarsh, it would appear that Norwich has certainly assisted in some manner.

Nevertheless, we are dealing with a person whose date of birth is the 8th August 1929 and is receiving ongoing nursing care. In our submission it is not the role of the Prison Service to provide nursing care but a role that should be for the National Health Service or, as is conceded that Mr. Biggs is clearly of no risk whatsoever to anyone including himself, he should properly be released on compassionate grounds.

You will note that in our letter to you we cited another client of ours, namely Ethel Anne Trigwell, who was sentenced for conspiracy to murder and was released after 11 years of a life sentence to a hospice. Of course it is conceded and understood that Miss Trigwell has sadly passed away and her illness was one of carcinoma. Her application was not so much one of a compassionate basis but an application which permitted the then Secretary of State and now Minister of Justice to release an inmate (a) that was of no danger to herself or the public and (b) to be able to die with dignity.

Mr. Biggs has suffered cerebrovascular accidents (strokes), he is undergoing PEG feeds, he suffers from hypertension, is on controlled medication, suffers from chronic gastric ulceration, has atrial fibrillation and in early 2007 had Catarectomy surgery. He uses a wheelchair at his own request and is unable to walk more than 100 paces without becoming seriously short of breath. He is unable to swallow and is fed through a gastric feed. He does of course enjoy some sensation such as ice cream when occasionally offered but of course even that carries a serious risk of aspiration (Phonetics) the release of a strong burst of air after some obstruents. He communicates with an alphabet board and non-verbal signs and whilst he has been assigned speech and language therapy, the matter has certainly not improved since his last medical report. The fact that he enjoys and has a sense of humour cannot be a factor which would preclude the Minister of Justice from applying his discretion for compassionate release.

In all the circumstances the Minister of Justice is dealing with an aged person with an aged and stale offence, with a man who surrendered himself when there was effectively no need and who may very well pass away whilst in custody which, in our submission, would be a considerable tragedy for all concerned.

We have received more than 10,000 letters of support, which we would be more than pleased to forward to the Minister of Justice, from all walks of life all supporting a compassionate release. We are of course aware that the Minister of Justice is concerned that in the event compassionate release is granted, concerns would be as to where he would effectively live and who would care for him. As you are aware, his son Michael attends and visits him regularly and will do all he possibly can to ensure that his father transcourses the rest of his days in peace and quiet and tranquillity and away from the media glare.

In our submission it is no concession or weakness in applying compassion to a person in this state and in any other of the European Union member states no one in this condition, including offences far more serious than the offence that Mr. Biggs was convicted of (without wishing to diminish the seriousness of the matter both in 1964 and today) but in any other State he would have been placed under home detention or in a proper hospital environment where he can effectively pass the final days, weeks, months, years, whatever remaining time in dignity. This certainly was achieved as far as Anne Trigwell was concerned but it is conceded that in her case the Minister of Justice was aware that she was suffering from cancer and that there was a limited period before it was expected that she would pass away. We do not wish to compare cases as our case must be taken on its own merits. It is of note that one of the Kray brothers was also released on a compassionate basis and he too subsequently passed away within the time frame that the then Secretary of State was made aware.

However, both the cases of Trigwell and Kray and others were dealing with offences of murder. In this case Mr. Biggs was convicted of 'conspiracy to stop mail with intent to rob' and 'robbery with aggravation'. His earliest parole date has been mercifully decided under the 'old' parole system being the 12th February 2010 but this is still two years away and, in all honesty, one wonders whether it is in the interests of justice and in the interests of the citizens of the UK and Mr. Biggs himself that he survives two more years and if he does, is it right that he should survive such under these conditions. A poll by the Daily Mail, notwithstanding a very negative article, showed that the majority of those members of the public whose opinion was sought were in favour of his compassionate release. It is not as if he has served no time whatsoever and without doubt the question of retribution has been addressed.

In our submission the application for compassionate release is based upon the final 'R' in the three R's criminal justice and sentencing:

1. Retribution.
2. Rehabilitation.
3. Redemption.

Mr. Biggs has certainly surpassed the retribution element of sentence and he is suffering by far more than anyone in different circumstances. As far as rehabilitation is concerned, there was never any question of this because over the past number of years Mr. Biggs has committed no criminal offences whatsoever. Even when he was in a desperate position

*for money to feed his son, he certainly did not fall foul of the law. That
leaves the element of redemption and, in our submission, it is not simply
redemption for him but redemption also for a society that jailed this man
for such a lengthy period of time and continues to impose that sentence
under the specific conditions as per the medical reports which are clearly
not compatible with prison.*

*In all the circumstances, our submission on behalf of Mr. Biggs is that he
should be released forthwith to the custody of his son Michael Biggs in
order that he transpires the remainder of his days in a law-abiding
manner and with a dignity that certain circumstances require. We will be
obliged if you will effect a decision as a matter of urgency.*

*Yours faithfully,
Studio Legale Internazionale
Giovanni di Stefano*

On 29 December 2007, the *New Zealand Herald/UK Independent* ran a
story on Ronnie's desperation to be free and live his last days with his
family:

*Ronnie Biggs, the Great Train Robber, made a desperate appeal for his
effort to get parole.*

*In a statement, Biggs, 78, asked to be released from jail to die with his
family: "I am an old man and often wonder if I truly deserve the extent
of my punishment? I have accepted it and only want freedom to die with
my family and not in jail. I hope Mr Straw decides to allow me to do that.*

*"I have been in jail for a long time and I want to die a free man. I am
sorry for what happened many years ago. It has not been an easy ride
over the years. Even in Brazil I was a prisoner of my own making," he
said.*

Biggs, who returned from Brazil in 2001 after 35 years on the run, is serving the 30-year sentence he was given in 1964 for his role in the theft of 2.6 million pounds - a record haul at the time.

A series of strokes has rendered him partially paralysed and unable to speak, and he is fed through a tube. He can however, walk unassisted and is mentally alert and in good humour.

His early release application forms show that his prison governor, James Shanley, has vetoed his request despite clearance from doctors, who say he is physically incapable of committing further crimes, and his probation officer, who is satisfied with his 34-year-old son Michael's plan to admit him to a private nursing home in Barnet, north London.

But Mr Shanley, the governor of category-C Norwich prison, where Biggs has 24-hour care, has kept him behind bars on the grounds that he is not about to die.

The doctor who compiled the medical report wrote: "Mr Biggs is unlikely to be capable of committing further criminal acts, particularly of a physical or violent or sexual nature."

His probation officer described how Biggs used an alphabet card to talk about his family, visiting and football, but never the 1963 train robbery that gained his notoriety.

Referring to Michael Biggs's plans for his father, he said: "These arrangements would seem suitable in terms of supervision, oversight and, as I understand, medical support."

But Mr Shanley, in answer to a question on the form "Do you consider that the prisoner should be released early?", writes: "No. There is little evidence that Mr Biggs is likely to die imminently and I do not think that he is incapacitated enough to not cope with the prison environment. HMP Norwich is able to adequately care for Mr Biggs."

Earlier this year Biggs, who has submitted several requests for release, was transferred to Norwich from the medical wing at London's high-security Belmarsh prison, where he has stayed since his return to the UK. He is not eligible for parole until 2010."

In an earlier statement, he apologised for his crime, claiming: "There is no honour to being known as a Great Train Robber. My life has been wasted."

His legal representative, Giovanni di Stefano, wrote to Jack Straw, the Secretary of State for Justice: "It is not the role of the Prison Service to provide nursing care but a role that should be for the National Health Service or, as it is conceded that Mr Biggs is clearly of no risk to anyone including himself, he should be released on compassionate grounds."

The Home Office declined to comment last week on Mr Biggs's request.

He's served ten years, so he's not getting away with anything. He's an old man who can't walk, can't talk and is no harm to anyone. How many appeals did Giovanni need to make before someone would listen and free him on compassionate grounds? Well, apparently at least one more was needed, as in February 2008 Giovanni received another knock-back:

The Secretary of State/Minister of Justice, call him what you will, has REFUSED our application for the compassionate release of Ronald Biggs for a second time. It seems that vendetta and retribution are the key words in the government of New Labour and Gordon Brown. Personally, I call it a frigging disgrace and probably unlawful. I am yet to be convinced that an 80-year-old man who was sentenced over 40 years ago can lawfully remain in jail on that sentence especially as he was clearly NOT produced at his appeal as was his right. I am thus going to write to the Lord Chief Justice on the matter. I had originally raised this issue with the then Vice President of the Court of Appeal, Criminal Division (Lord Justice Rose) who saw no purpose in the matter. Of course, but Rose LJ has been the cause of more injustices in the criminal justice system that Prof. Spilsbury! So I won't stop fighting for Ronnie Biggs. Further, the Home Office/Ministry of Justice have ignored over 10,000 letters from individuals asking and petitioning for the compassionate release of Ronnie Biggs. Both Straw and Smith should put a mask over their faces in shame, but then again they already have a dozen or more on other matters so one more one less won't matter to them. A day of infamy in my view and if Ronnie Biggs dies in jail then the British Government will truly see what a backlash there will be, not just from me but from the average everyday person in the street. (Giovanni di Stefano, 12 February 2008)

Of course, Giovanni wasn't the only one keeping Ronnie's plight at the forefront of everyone's minds and fighting for justice and freedom, and in February 2008 Tel Currie e-mailed the following press release to Mal, Web Master of Dave Courtney's website.

I fear for the morality of this great nation of ours. A nation that has been through so much in the last century and has been forced to take up arms to avoid oppression on more than one occasion. Now, it would appear governments are admiring and even copying the oppressor rather than the lessons that can be learned from the oppressed. Must justice now revolve around the idea of crushing a man's spirit and then waiting hauntingly and ghoulishly whilst looking at their watches for the body literally to be crushed as well? Will they not clock off until a man is buried deep in the earth, a technique rejected by even the most barbaric of countries?

What more can a slow grinding system do to Ronnie Biggs? Even the dimmest of us knows this system has ground itself so hard it has dug, stumbled and fallen into a hole it cannot climb out of! We all know the only idea they actually have is to wait for Ronnie Biggs to die. This is not just desserts, it's a complete lack of imagination and ideas.

This inspiring system was used on Reggie Kray. The system killed Reg Kray. The correct check-ups and treatment would have diagnosed cancer in time to save him. I, for one, refuse to believe they wanted to save him.

His death solved too many problems for them to resist; it was a glorious open goal that even the worst striker in the world would have made sure he did not miss even with his weak foot!

So they told him it was nothing to worry about and for crippling stomach pain gave him two paracetamol at a time, an amount I wouldn't bother with even for the mildest of headaches!

Then, when it was too late, up jumped a cancer diagnosis! Oh dear, where could that've come from? ... Whoops-a-daisy.

The system has Reg Kray's blood on its hands and the people responsible are probably rather proud of it.

Now we have the same ingenious method being used on Ronnie Biggs. The difference between Reg and Ronnie Biggs is huge. Biggsy was no real villain, he was a desperate man who was skint. He was not feared like Reg because A) that's not in him and B) he was a carpenter NOT a gangster. He was not a threat to society then, so what does that make him now?

Like Bronson, Kevin Lane and Razor Smith, Biggs is a non-killer, unlike the government who keeps them in jail for being naughty! How many young men and women have politicians killed over the years? Ha! Ha! ... It's almost funny ... almost. It's like Peter Sutcliffe putting you in prison for GBH!!!

Think of those who unleash hell on Iraq and Afghanistan, then think of a near 80-year-old man who can't talk and has had numerous strokes who sat in a lorry watching an unarmed robbery over 40 years ago and has never hurt a sausage. Who's the evil party here? Well the old bloke obviously! He obviously has no morals. "Ooops ... sorry that was a civilian shelter we blew up but isn't that Ronnie Biggs a nasty man, isn't Charlie Bronson violent?"Violent????? Ha! Ha! Ha! Good one!

The warmongers obviously don't think we are intelligent enough to work out what they are doing. The fact that a brain dead lemming with amnesia could work it out is more a reflection on them than us. It would *surely be a vote winner if, whilst invading the world, the system also showed a small capability for compassion by letting an old man out of prison over forty years after his extremely minor part in a crime.*

Mr politician, we are not that stupid. Show some imagination, show some compassion, show some justice and you might ... just might ... regain some of the respect you lost years ago. (Tel Currie, 24 February 2008)

Mal is a Web Master extraordinaire and deserves huge thanks for his contribution to Ronnie's campaign. Mal, you have supported us all the way and have always uploaded our 'Biggsy news' onto the relevant websites that you controlled at the time and still do. Not only do you upload the text news, but also your software skills are obviously your strong point as you find photos, previous illustrations and even media web-based videos to accompany the stories, which makes them so much more interesting and the message even more powerful. Thank you for your brilliant support.

Ronnie had been in HMP Norwich just nine months when Giovanni told the UK/world media that he could still be free for Christmas 2008. He had another ace up his sleeve. Giovanni had written to the Parole Board requesting his release, pointing out that under Section 60 of the Criminal Justice Act prisoners sentenced to a fixed-term imprisonment should be considered for parole after having served one-third of any prison sentence. As of that date, 4 April 2008, Ronnie had served 3,385 days in custody and Giovanni therefore believed that Ronnie should be considered by the Parole Board for release on 25 December 2008, as a matter of law not discretion. Also, although Ronnie was sentenced in April 1964, three years before the parole scheme was introduced, Giovanni held that it should still apply as Ronnie's co-defendants had all been released on parole. This was Giovanni's submission:

129

4 April 2008
DMGDS/SLI/MS/BIGGS
AN0082

Mr. James Hough,
Release & Recall Section,
Directorate of the National Offender Manager,
Room 135 Abell House,
John Islip Street,
London, SWIP 4LH

Dear Sir,

Re: Ronald Arthur BIGGS

We refer to our previous correspondence in the above matter and acknowledge that yet again the Minister of Justice has declined to interfere with the sentence of our client by virtue of applying S.36(1) of the Criminal Justice Act 1991 for compassionate release. There is, however, another matter which in our respectful submission allows the Minister of Justice proper and lawful intervention. We are thus sending a copy of this letter to the Chairman of the Parole Board and to the Governor of HMP Norwich.

It is our submission that our client is entitled by law to be considered for release on parole within the next 265 days from the date of this letter. We submit such on the basis that our client is entitled to be considered for parole under the Criminal Justice Act 1967 s.60 as all other members of the so-called 'Great Train Robbery Gang', namely after a third of any sentence elapsed. We provide for your attention the relevant dates:

Introduction

1. Mr. Ronald Arthur Biggs was convicted on 14th April 1964 for his part in the 'Great Train Robbery'. He was sentenced to a total of 30 years imprisonment.

2. He was arrested on Wednesday, 4th September 1963 and remained in custody until his escape from detention on Thursday, 8th July 1965. That calculates a total of 673 days in custody.

3. On Friday 1st February 1974 our client was arrested in Brazil on an application for extradition but released from prison in Brasilia on Monday 6th May 1974. That calculates a total of 94 days in custody.

4. On Monday, 16th March 1981 our client was 'kidnapped' by a gang that took him to Bridgetown in Barbados where he was arrested on an application for extradition but released on Friday, 24th April 1974. That calculates a total of 94 days in custody.

5. Our client returned to the jurisdiction of his own volition after in 1997 the British Government 'gave up' any further extradition attempt. On the 7th May 2001 our client surrendered himself and has been in custody to date and as of today this calculates a total of 2,524 days in custody. The total days our client has thus been in custody as a result of the sentence imposed upon him is 3,385 days in custody.

Our client was sentenced in 1964 and at that time no parole existed within English legislation. In 1967 the Criminal Justice Act s.60 was applied as those prisoners that were subject to a sentence of fixed term imprisonment were considered for parole after having served one third of any sentence. As stated previously, all of the co-defendants of our client benefited from such and were released on parole.

As the sentence of our client imposed was 30 years, our client thus should serve 10 years, namely 3,650 days prior to release on license if the Parole Board and circumstances would warrant.

Our client, notwithstanding having evaded justice, is entitled to be considered for parole under the system of parole that was applicable at the time when parole first was introduced. The British Government made a number of extradition requests finally conceding in 1997. Had any of those requests been successful, especially the request of 1974 to the Brazilian Authorities, our client would have benefited then as did his co-defendants from the parole system as it then was.

In our most respectful submission our client having surrendered to custody on his own volition, especially when the British Government had conceded that no further requests would be contemplated, he held a legitimate expectation (a) to be returned to jail to complete his sentence, which is the case and more important (b) to be considered for parole or early release under s.60 of the Criminal Justice Act 1967. It cannot be that a sentence of 30 years, as may have been appropriate in 1963, is not subject to appeal because it was the 'appropriate sentence of the time' notwithstanding that today it is unlikely a sentence of more than 15 years could be sustained yet our client must be subject to the new parole 'system' which increases the time that one spends in jail.

In our submission the Parole Board must be moved to consider the release of our client with 265 days from today at the earliest possible date, namely Thursday, 25th December 2008.

We thus ask that the Parole Board immediately commence considerations in order that no delays occur and we would also very kindly request your confirmation that our client will be considered for parole release on the date we have specified based upon our calculations which we have taken from the official records.

Finally, we kindly request a speedy decision in this matter taking into account the condition, frailty and age of Mr. Biggs. It would be nothing short of a tragedy if Mr. Biggs were to die in custody.

We thank you in advance for your kind consideration.

Yours sincerely

STUDIO LEGALE INTERNAZIONALE

GIOVANNI DI STEFANO

As with anything legal, it all takes time, and June was now approaching. Giovanni and his team again made worldwide headlines with "Train Robber Ronnie's hope nearing". Giovanni stated that the Ministry had sent Ronnie's case to the Parole Board for consideration of a July 2009 release, although he had previously been pressing for a December 2008 release date, taking into account the time Ronnie had spent in custody in Brazil and Barbados before his 2001 UK return. On hearing the news, Ronnie told his son Michael that he could finally see the end of his nightmare now that common sense seemed to have prevailed.

I sent Giovanni an account of my visit to see Ronnie in June 2008, as I was in regular touch with him and liked to keep him updated on Ronnie's condition following my visits and also passed on any news received in letters from Ron, and he kindly posted it on his website to keep Ronnie's supporters informed:

13 June 2008

I AM PUBLISHING A LETTER RECEIVED FROM MIKE GRAY, WHO HAS JUST BEEN TO SEE RONNIE BIGGS. THE LETTER SPEAKS FOR ITSELF!!!

Good evening from the UK. I hope you are on your way home as you read this. Be careful if Bush is about.

Visited Ronnie on Tuesday (June 10th) in HMP Norwich. As it was a mid-week visit, the hall was only occupied by 5 visits, a bit different to the 50 plus in Belmarsh.

Ronnie was wheeled in last as usual. Whether it's because he's the only inmate from the Healthcare Unit, or whether it's Home Office tactics to reduce the visiting time, who knows. I believe it's the latter. His cheeky grin said it all, letting the Prison Officers wheel him in as though he's Royalty. I'm sure they hate it. He certainly loved it.

Apart from Ronnie, as usual the average age of the others in the hall was only 20-25. Ronnie has no one to communicate with and therefore it's very difficult to rehabilitate him, especially if most of the YOs (Young Offenders) don't even know who he is.

Ronnie was very smart and immaculate in appearance - close shave, Ben Sherman shirt and new watch, both of which he bought from the Argos catalogue, which is available to inmates. Upon my arrival, Ronnie spelt out on his A-Z laminated A4 sheet that he was pleased to tell me that his visits have now been increased to TWO hours, as opposed to the one hour. The Governor introduced the two hour visits for ALL inmates not just Ronnie, but it is as it was in HMP Hellmarsh (Belmarsh). I was pleased as the journey to Norwich is not the easiest for me, and the extra hour was very well received by both Ronnie and myself.

I was asking him as many questions as possible, so he could exercise his fingers on the laminated sheet, and also it keeps his mind sharp and active. Although Ronnie's body might be slowly giving up on him, his mind certainly is not.

After discussing you, his first wife Charmian in Australia, pals in Brazil, money, his health, the screws, amongst many other things, he was most interested in 'gun crime' on our streets, saying he doesn't know how people go about their everyday lives with the constant fear of being shot or stabbed. He said it reminded him of the Rio De Janeiro backstreets and nightlife, where murders became the norm.

He's still being fed via a tube through the stomach (liquids) and he knows that will never change, but his new doctor (female) is looking after him very well. Also he now has someone to write his letters and VOs for him. He referred to him as The Sweaty Sock. I said to tell The Sock, that WE all appreciate his help in keeping Ronnie in communication with us all, and if he lets me know who he is I'm sure a thank you gift at some stage would be appreciated.

Ronnie cannot have his false teeth in anymore, as his saliva was causing problems on his mouth/lips, therefore the doctor has told him not to have his teeth in, and Ronnie is pleased that he no longer has to constantly dribble in front of visitors, which was a full-time job for myself, wiping his mouth on visits. Ronnie still has his dignity and is a very proud person on appearance and health issues.

I left him at 4.10 p.m., with tears from Ron as usual. He does get very emotional, and he knows that we all love him and are doing all we possibly can to get him that all important Parole date.

Ronnie is 79 on August 8th, and we all hope and pray that it's his last birthday in captivity.

Before I could get to leave the hall, I turned around and Ronnie was gone. In the past they have not wanted all the other visitors to chat to him on the way out, so I have often wondered why they keep placing him next to the entry/exit door, as it's obvious people want to say hello to the man, whom I believe is being slowly crucified on the Home Office cross ...

God bless you, Giovanni, you are our ONLY hope,

Take care, your friend,

Mike

MIKE GRAY

ORGANISER

FREE RONNIE BIGGS CAMPAIGN

Giovanni di Stefano posted the following Biggsy story on his website from his mobile phone while he was in Iraq on business. As usual, wherever Giovanni is, Ronnie is not far from his thoughts.

6 July 2008

SUNDAY PEOPLE ARTICLE: BIGGS BACK IN COURT EXCLUSIVE

Ronnie on show after 7 years plea for new sentence cut.

Ronnie Biggs will arrive in court in a wheelchair this week as his lawyers fight to win his early release. The Great Train Robber, 78, has asked to sit *in on the hearing. It will be one of his few appearances in public since he was locked up seven years ago after returning to Britain after 35 years on the run.*

Parole chiefs already say frail Biggs - sentenced to 30 years in 1964 for his part in the £2.6 million mail train heist - can be released in July next year. His lawyers will go to St Albans Crown Court, Herts, on Thursday to ask for 94 days to be slashed from his remaining time inside. That's how long he spent in custody in Brazil and Barbados awaiting extradition after ending his exile in Rio.

Biggs, who escaped jail in 1965, is now in Belmarsh prison, southeast London.

His lawyer Giovanni Di Stefano said: "Biggs is almost 80. It's time for the old guy to go home."

A legal source said last night: "It is quite unusual for Ronnie to be taken from custody to attend this type of hearing but it's something he wants to do. The judge will see how weak and frail he is."

The accompanying message from Giovanni read:

We are actually looking for almost six months back to count as remission for parole purposes. The Home Office have accepted my submissions in law that the old law counts for Ronnie (I personally wish to thank the Minister of Justice for this, Jack Straw QC). In my view, however, his time that he was awaiting an extradition decision (namely the 90 days x 2 in Brazil and Barbados) he was NOT 'unlawfully at large' because he was in custody and that in my view should count for parole purposes. This matter is governed by the Criminal Justice Act 1967 and CJA 1991 but it is a discretionary matter which only a judge (in my view) can deal with, although the Minister has some say ... maybe. You see the matter is complicated by the fact (I must be honest about this) I can't have my whole cake and eat it. ... I have successfully pleaded that Ronnie must be dealt with by the old law; well the old law made it discretionary upon a judge regarding time spent abroad awaiting extradition. Now the law today makes it obligatory that time spent abroad awaiting extradition counts towards sentence and today the Home Office have really no say in sentencing matters but when Ronnie was sentenced they did! Do you see our dilemma??? So we will do our best ...

Government officials contacted Giovanni on 10 July 2008, stating that Ronnie could possibly be freed on parole earlier than the suggested July 2009 date due his custody periods in Brazil and Barbados. This would bring his release date forward to February 2009, but not just any old February date - Valentine's Day, 14 February. The Parole Board still had to agree to the overseas custody inclusion, but Giovanni was cautiously optimistic and Ronnie was over the moon at the prospect of an earlier release date.

It's early August and that's how the situation stands. We are all awaiting official confirmation, or otherwise, of the Valentine's Day release date. If the earlier date isn't approved, then we will all wait for the expiration of the legal term of another five months to see Ronnie coming through the main gate of HMP Norwich in his wheelchair. I suspect he could be giving the 'finger' in true Biggsy style!

Chapter 9
The Good, the Bad
and the Birthday
(by Mike Gray)

Tel Currie earlier this year (2008) suggested the idea of writing a book on the story of Ronnie Biggs - the real Ronnie Biggs, not the Ronnie Biggs that most people seem to think they know, i.e. the one in Brazil with a beer, or the one on the cover of an Ex- Pistols record saying, "Bollocks to you, Ma'am", or the old crippled bloke who came back to the UK to ponce off the NHS and have untold beers in Margate; or the one who would get placed in a cushy open prison for a few months, then sell his story - or one he's made up - and then fuck off back to Brazil, where he can live in absolute luxury; or the one who's got lots of Great Train Robbery dosh hidden away, so when he kicks the bucket (passes away to those of you from a privileged background) he can leave it all in his will to his son Mikey, who will then in turn become a multimillionaire and live out the rest of his life with his family in near-paradise ... "Not guilty, your honour," is my stern response to those people who think I have just described Ronnie Biggs's life in a paragraph, the same idiots who still believe he should rot in jail forever. Well, after all, he coshed the train driver 20 times, he was the ringleader on the robbery (move over, Brucey Baby), he was in on his own kidnap to get even more money, he sang with the Sex Pistols because he thought they were his sons - after all, Biggsy has about 30 sons in this world ... Blah, blah, blah, talk about a broken record. I feel like snapping the needle on that one!

Throughout my 30-plus years involved with Ronnie Biggs, I have come across so many so-called TV/film celebrities that sought out Ronnie when he was in Rio, Brazil, and was totally skint - his son Michael will tell you how skint they became. These were people with CVs packed with music awards, TV and film awards and all their household names plus baggage, but they ALL went looking for Ronald Arthur Biggs because he was great press and they could apparently benefit by saying (as many of them did), "I know a villain/robber/gangster/underworld character … I have connections, so watch out" etc. Yes, you know who you are - and so do I, because I have tried to contact many of you over the past 6 to 10 years to say, "How about you helping Ronnie this time, now he's back in the UK?" But, as I thought, either no reply came back or a very poor excuse. Dear readers of this book, I am sure you will be very surprised with the following list of 'celebrities' who sought out Ronnie Biggs in Brazil - for what? How, in their profession, can being photographed or interviewed with an old has-been Train Robber in Brazil be beneficial to their career? You decide. As for me, I cannot understand why they did it, because when Ronnie returned in 2001 they didn't want to know him at all.

• The Police (Sting). They played a gig in Rio de Janeiro and Ronnie was seen, and is shown in a previous Ronnie Biggs book, allegedly teaching Sting how to play guitar.

• Maxi Priest (reggae singer). He met with Ronnie and they discussed how they were both Brixton Boys and also carpenters.

• Anthea Turner (TV presenter). She called in on Ron after he twisted his ankle at the carnival and he had it in plaster, Why?

• The Happy Mondays (Shaun Ryder and Bez) called round to Ronnie's villa, giving him a plastic copper's hat and Arsenal T-shirt. Guys, I have tried to contact you lot for so long about helping Ronnie but no response.

• Steve Jones and Paul Cook (Ex-Pistols) - nothing as expected.

• Ozzy Osborne. You invited Ronnie to your Rio hotel for lunch -

your photograph is in one of Ronnie's books. But my 10-plus letters to your UK home must be lost in the post (Royal Mail, eh? Maybe someone nicked the mailbags?).

• British Leyland Mini. You used Ronnie on an advertising poster in 1977 and said if Biggs wanted to take you to court then he should come home. Well, he's home now, so where are Ronnie's royalties?

• Geoff Deane (*Biggsy's Bible*). Didn't you agree to send Ronnie at least £3,000 when the book was published in 1988? Ronnie has still not heard from you, Geoff.

One of my favourite UK actors is Mr Larry Lamb. Since the '70s days when he starred in *The Fox Family*, he has become one of the UK's most famous actors, and Larry also has a 'Train Robbers' connection. Although at the moment he stars in *Eastenders* alongside the brilliant Barbara Windsor, Larry played (and very much looked like) Ronnie Biggs in a BBC adaptation play called *The Great Paper Chase*, a docudrama based around Scotland Yard's pathetic attempt to bring Ronnie home from Rio de Janeiro in 1974. He later appeared on the big screen in the brilliant film (with a superb soundtrack) *Buster* (1988), this time playing Bruce Reynolds, the Great Train Robbery mastermind, alongside Phil Collins as Ronald Buster Edwards. Another actor who deserves greater accolades is Ralph Brown, who played Ronnie Biggs in *Buster*. Paul Freeman was excellent as Ronnie Biggs in the film *The Prisoner of Rio* and Biggsy actually got himself a cameo role in the film - if you watch the beginning you might just see him talking to Paul Freeman. It tells the story of Ronnie's kidnap and what happened to Michael Biggs while Ronnie was held captive, and has since become very rare and collectable.

I am still receiving regular e-mails from the Pickstons in Brazil, telling me that Ronnie's old drinking buddies in Santa Theresa still miss him and cannot wait for his return - that's Johnny and The Blind Policeman. Ronnie still laughs about them on our visits. Johnny also pointed out that the owner of his favourite bar (Bar Doarnaudo, Santa Theresa), still keeps going on about Ronnie owing him 10 dollars after all these years!

Today (8 August) is Ronnie's 79th birthday, and the UK press have kept a low profile on the story - very unusual, especially as this is going to be Ronnie's last birthday behind bars, whether he's released in February or July 2009. The next birthday will be the biggs-est as he'll be 80 years old and, more importantly, also a free man. This certainly will be an event that the UK press/media will be sniffing around, looking for an invite to the year's largest celebrity-gangster party. Don't forget, readers, you read and heard about it here. In fact, why not bring this book with you and get it signed by famous celebrities of the music, television and film worlds - and, of course, the underworld.

I mailed Ronnie his usual birthday card with a train on it. This is something I have done for many years for both birthdays and Christmas, although finding Christmas cards with a train theme can be quite difficult. However, Ronnie has been known to get moody if a card arrives without a train on it ... all aboard.

Ronnie celebrated his 79th birthday in HMP Norwich with a visit from his son Michael, and is still waiting to hear whether the Home Office are going to allow the Parole Board a release date of February or July 2009. Either way, it's only a few months away and Ronnie will continue to show his strength and mental alertness and validate himself as a model prisoner.

A Press Association release was issued on Ronnie's 79th Birthday, entitled "Biggs' Lawyer Blasts Vindictive Britain", which said:

Great Train Robber Ronnie Biggs' lawyer Giovanni di Stefano called Britain a "vindictive state" today for not releasing the 80 year old. [wrong - he's 79!]
As the 45th Anniversary of the Great Train Robbery (8th August 1963) approaches, Biggs' lawyer Giovanni di Stefano said Britain was "vindictive and favours the rich. Perhaps if Mr Biggs still had his fortune things may have been different for him." Earlier this month Mr di Stefano headed a

campaign to release Biggs early, stating that the time he spent in prison abroad should be counted against his sentence. He succeeded. He said that the Parole Board would now review his imprisonment in February, rather than June next year (2009).

"There are three R's to crime and punishment: Retribution, Rehabilitation and Redemption" he said. "Ronnie Biggs falls into all three categories. If you can redeem a mortgage you can redeem a man. He is a seriously ill man who has suffered three strokes, he cannot go to the toilet on his own, and he should have been released long ago. Compassion in England is limited and it is a crying shame that British lawyers have not appealed to release him perhaps as passionately as I have, but then we Europeans look at the law in a different manner. We look at the law more than the facts and it is the application of the law as submitted by me that has conquered the facts." When asked why he had been campaigning for Mr Biggs' release for so long, he said, "Mr Biggs doesn't even know this yet, but I met him in Brazil in 1973 when I was a young boy long before he was identified by a newspaper journalist. All I saw was a nice man. I uphold him as an example of what a single father should be. I have been one too in my time and it's not easy. I have been working for so long, for free, simply because he was just a nice man."

It continued to state, as so many national newspapers do, that Ronnie Biggs left the UK on the run via Spain and Australia to Brazil, but that's not correct - Ronnie never went to Spain. This is a case of our UK media getting Ronnie Biggs mixed up with the other Ronnie (no, not Barker in *Porridge!*), i.e. the legend that is Mr Ronnie Knight, who went on the run to Spain and, like Freddie Foreman before him, was dragged back to the UK by Scotland Yard. Di Stefano added that Ronnie was ecstatic at the prospect of his release next year and that he wasn't angry, he just wanted to die a free man - that was his dream.

The above press release was uploaded onto Giovanni di Stefano's website, where you can also sign the Ronnie Biggs petition. As of August 2008, a total of 8,652 people have signed the petition so far. The link has a very prominent position on the home page and reads:

> *"Ronnie Biggs is being pump fed in his prison cell. We the undersigned by our hand affirm and sign this petition for the release from imprisonment of Ronald Arthur Biggs, born on the 8th August 1929, and sentenced on the 15th April 1964 to a term of 30 years by Mr Justice Edmund Davies at Aylesbury Assizes, and do request of our Sovereign an act of clemency and to sign the instrument known as the prerogative of mercy causing the said Ronald Arthur Biggs to be released forthwith."*

Over the years, and especially since 2001, I have been in regular e-mail contact with Mr Uri Geller, as mentioned earlier in the book. Uri met Ronnie in Rio de Janeiro in the late '90s and they became, and still are, firm friends. I have always kept Uri updated on Ronnie's condition, as I do with all the other people/supporters on the campaign database (i.e. Charlie Breaker, Johnny in Brazil, Charmian in Australia, Mike Cunnington in Australia, Brian Running in whatever part of the world he's in, and many, many others. Without fail Uri always responds to my e-mail with a thank you or a get well/positive message for Ronnie and me.

On 14 August 2008 I received an e-mail from Uri, as I had previously told him about the book and had asked if he would like to say a few words about Ronnie and the background to their friendship. He said he was delighted to oblige and was happy for me to include the following post, which was given pride of place on his website in May 2001 upon Ronnie's return to the UK and also featured in the *Daily Mirror*:

> *When Ronnie Biggs flew into Britain last week, his weak health saddened me. I met him in Rio seven years ago, a strong, vital man with a face damaged by heavy drinking. He had broken his foot and wanted me to*

heal it - I told him that he was the healer, and all I could do was act as the catalyst, to trigger his own healing energies. Biggs was an intelligent man behind the bad man's bluster, and he intuitively understood what I was saying. He assumed a relaxed pose and closed his eyes, focusing his imagination on a mended bone in a healthy foot. After a while he said, without opening his eyes: "I ain't thinking of my foot no more. Know what I'm thinking of? A pint of best." "So imagine that you are walking into an English pub," I said, "without your stick, your foot free from pain. And you go up to the bar and put that foot on the rail and order that pint of best, and when you drink it down in one swallow the dark brown liquid turns gold and flows through your bones into your foot. And there is great strength in your foot, and the love you have for that beer fills your foot and energises it." I always encourage people during healing sessions to let the emotions take control. Ronnie was passionate about that picture of a warm pint, which symbolised his intense homesickness. By harnessing that strength of feeling, he was able to release powerful healing energies. By the next time I visited his hillside home above Rio, a few days later, the bone was knitting well. Ronnie Biggs always knew he'd come back to England. I knew it too, when I heard him talk of that pint. I hope he gets it.

On 16 August there was another Biggs birthday - Michael's 34th, so I called him to wish him a happy birthday. He had just flown back from Brazil on business. As always, he seemed to be working every hour that God sent to make a better and more comfortable life for himself and his lovely family, wife Veronica and daughter Ingrid, who have settled into the suburban lifestyle in North London in their attractive terraced home. It only seemed like yesterday that I was reading the UK newspaper stories about Ronnie being safe and eligible to remain in Brazil as a result of his girlfriend Raimunda giving birth to a bouncing baby boy called Michael.

On the following day, Michael Biggs made a fresh media plea for his father to be released from Norwich Prison before he dies, explaining, "He is in incredibly bad health. He has had heart attacks and strokes and we feel he should be released. Dad has to be fed via a tube and only communicates via a spelling board. I'm not even allowed to take a photo of him. It's clear the Government doesn't want the public to see how he looks. For the crime he committed, we feel he has done enough." Michael's daughter Ingrid was also planning to write to the Parole Board to see if he could be released in time for her ninth birthday on 22 January 2009.

Michael today has his own website, which is very informative and is not all about his father or the Great Train Robbery, but more about Michael and his life, loves and ambitions. You can contact him or listen to his music, which includes some superb snippets of his Brazilian funk records as well as full details about his Brazilian band, who play regularly in central London at Brazilian clubs where everyone is welcome.

And don't forget to check out Michael's youtube video of 'Daddy was a Train Robber', which was shot in November 2007 at The Beauchamp Pub in Knightsbridge. Michael and his record producer neighbour Keith 'Dickie' Finch and the band set up in the boozer and the song was played over and over while the filming took place. As the early evening recording turned into a late and then even later evening recording and filming, a few of the London underworld arrived and if you look closely at the video you can spot them ... or can you?

The afternoon was a great laugh and the pub was open as per usual to all regulars and anyone who wanted a beer, even during filming. I arrived at The Beauchamp around 1 p.m. and was surprised to see the pub fairly empty as the lunchtime trade started to return to the offices for the afternoon, but the characters left behind, to the average person in the street, could be described as a bit shifty-looking. Having said that, I was wearing my suit and black shirt, with a Crombie coat on my arm, so no doubt I looked like a dodgy bastard too! I wondered if they were the extras for the filming, but anyway I grabbed a beer (The Beauchamp does

145

a superb pint of bitter) and sat and relaxed. Just as Ronnie Kray used to do so in The Grave Maurice pub in Bethnal Green, I took up a seat where I could see everyone coming into the pub and leaving.

After an hour or so, lots of people started to arrive. I started speaking to a lovely fella (in the video with his beige Crombie and large cigar) looking every inch a gangster, and as he towered over me he introduced me to his young lady, whom I recognised as Jennie Matthias, the lead singer of The Belle Stars. She has a superb soulful voice and I believe she should be a megastar today. We chatted about music, Michael and, of course, the legend Mr Ronnie Biggs. It was so heart-warming to hear comments about Ronnie that reflected my own personal feelings and beliefs about Ron. It goes without saying that we all got on like a house on fire, and although it was only 2 p.m. in the afternoon at that point, we were all still chatting and smoking on the Knightsbridge pavements well into late evening. We all loved the ska/reggae sound, so we talked about that for hours.

Jennie knew Michael Biggs' neighbour Keith 'Dickie' Finch very, very well, as he was her record producer. Dickie's record company/band are called JA13 and the band members are Keith Finch, Alex Charlie Finch, Debra Barker, Chico Chagas, Michael Biggs, and guests. Dickie Finch describes the JA13 sound as "Mayhem. We've taken all the influences of what we like over the past 40 years of music and melted it in. We have classical music mixed with ska, we have dub mixed with samba; there are no rules, as we are not searching to please. We are an art movement not a money business. We hope people like, or appreciate, it, but if you don't there's plenty out there for everyone."

As Michael Biggs and the band arrived I also recognised the very talented Debra Barker, also from The Belle Stars. Debra sang on the vocals of 'Daddy was a Train Robber' and features in the video. As they set up the band, the pub seemed to fill very quickly. Press and media people were also arriving and it looked like being a long night. "Another please," I found myself repeating over and over again. As the 'Train Robber' recording started and stopped and started again, it helped to have four or five beers inside you!

Michael, always the perfect gentleman (as his dad has always taught him), approached me and after the double-cheek kiss and infamous Brazilian hug he introduced me to everyone that had arrived. We were all there for one reason, and one reason only - to raise public and worldwide awareness for Ronnie Biggs by way of a video/record, which was produced by the incredible and very nice guy and top man Mr Rick Stax - even though I ended up telling him that I wrote the original 'Train Robber' lyrics in the Gents toilet at the Beauchamp.

Then the door opened and in walked Jimmy (Jamal) Shreim, whom I hadn't seen for a few years. He was a neighbour and very close family friend of Ronnie and Michael, and it was Jimmy who told me that when he and Ronnie used to play pool in Ronnie's house, just as Ronnie was about to pot for the game, his old-fashioned fax machine would kick into action and out would spew a few fax sheets from me! Cheers, Jim, you are a true, loyal pal and I appreciate your friendship.

As the recording reached the halfway point, I was stood by the door and in walked Mr Freddie Foreman. I embraced Freddie, as usual, and his first words were, "Fuck me, you're the only fella I recognise!" Most of the pub was brimming with musicians and press journalists. It was very satisfying to hear that from Freddie, whom I'd last seen eight months earlier at Joey Pyle's funeral, together with his son Jamie. I took Fred to the Bar to buy him a lager and then told Michael that Fred was in the house, by which time the press had recognised the legend that is Freddie 'Brown Bread' Foreman and surrounded him with camera lights and microphones. The most important factor, however, was that I gave Fred his pint of lager! Fred soon got well into the mood of the Biggsy evening and he can be seen singing along with all of us on the video. Freddie, as a close friend of Ronnie Biggs, has always given the Free Ronnie Biggs campaign 100% support. Fred, you're a real diamond.

Poor old Tel Currie couldn't make the recording, as he had fallen down the stairs at home and had broken his leg in two places - painful or what? It was a real shame, as it would've made the evening just a bit more special if Tel had been present.

It's now 24 August, and as I am writing the closing paragraphs of this book, an e-mail has dropped into my inbox from Giovanni di Stefano to let me know that he is okay and safe, although he is still on business in Iraq with suicide bombs going off all around him, but he assured me that he would be in touch with us on his return to Rome. Again, Ronnie is never far from his thoughts and if anyone can clinch the best deal for Biggsy, he can, and he will never give up until a satisfactory conclusion is reached - and neither will his devoted family, friends and supporters.

Tel and I decided to write this book to reveal the inside story of Ronnie's shocking treatment in Her Majesty's institutions since his arrival back in his homeland, England, in May 2001 to the current day. We, and all Ronnie's supporters, hope that his 'slow crucifixion on the Home Office cross' is now coming to an end and he can live out the rest of his days a free man with his devoted family in peace and dignity.

God bless you, Ron, We love you, and you know it.

Mike Gray & Tel Currie

OTHER BOOKS BY TEL CURRIE

Bouncers by Tel Currie & Julian Davies

Heroes & Villains by Tel Currie & Charlie Bronson

WEBSITES TO VISIT:

www.freebronson.co.uk

www.thekrays.co.uk

www.badboybooks.co.uk

www.Michaelbiggs.com

www.davecourtney.com

www.jasonmarinner.com

www.gangstervideos.com

OTHER CRIME BOOKS
PUBLISHED BY APEX:

THE LOOSE SCREW
by Jim Dawkins
£10.00
ISBN: 978-1-906358-01-3

**THE BRITISH CRIME AND
PRISON QUIZ BOOK**
by Jim Dawkins and Dave Courtney
£7.99
ISBN: 978-1-906358-01-3

**WARRIOR KINGS:
THE SOUTH LONDON GANG WARS 1976-1982**
by Noel 'Razor' Smith
£7.99
ISBN: 978-1-904444-95-4

NIL DESPERANDUM: "NEVER DESPAIR"
by Terry Smith
£7.99
ISBN: 978-1-904444-83-1

LOONYOLOGY
by Charles Bronson
£18.99
ISBN: 978-1-906358-11-2